S0-DTL-493

Four York Railways Birney cars, one on a National Railway Historical Society charter trip, meet at The Square in downtown York, Pa., Dec. 1, 1935.

Keystone State Traction

PENNSYLVANIA'S HISTORIC TROLLEY SYSTEMS

ROBERT G. LEWIS
WITH HOWARD L. STEVENS
AND WILLIAM C. VANTUONO

BULLETIN 142 OF THE CENTRAL ELECTRIC RAILFANS' ASSOCIATION

Keystone State Traction

PENNSYLVANIA'S HISTORIC TROLLEY SYSTEMS

By Robert G. Lewis, with Howard L. Stevens and William C. Vantuono

BULLETIN 142 OF THE CENTRAL ELECTRIC RAILFANS' ASSOCIATION

©2009 by the Central Electric Railfans' Association
An Illinois Not-for-Profit Corporation
P.O. Box 503, Chicago, IL 60690-0503, U.S.A.

2008 CERA DIRECTORS

J. Terrell Colson	Anthony Coppoletta
Graham C. Garfield	Daniel D. Joseph
Walter R. Keevil	Dennis McClendon
Bruce G. Moffat	Joseph L. Reuter
Jeffrey L. Wien	Paul F. Willer

All rights reserved. No part of this book may be commercially reproduced or utilized in any form, except for brief quotations, nor by any means electronic or mechanical, including photocopying and recording, nor by any informational storage/retrieval system, without permission in writing from the Central Electric Railfans' Association.

Keystone State Traction was edited and designed by William C. Vantuono. Production was coordinated by Bruce G. Moffat.

CERA Bulletins are technical, educational references prepared as historic projects by members of the Central Electric Railfans' Association, working without salary due to their interest in the subject. This bulletin is consistent with the stated purpose of the corporation: To foster the study of the history, equipment, and operation of electric railways.

ISBN: 978-0-915348-42-8
Library of Congress Control Number: 2008938148

Dedication

T o my brother Hansell, who inspired and encouraged my love of railways.

The year is 1928. The location is the Rancocas Moulding Sand Company in Centerton, N.J. Robert G. Lewis, age 12 (at right, in the cab) and Hansell Lewis, age 15, play pretend trainmen in an ancient 0-4-0 teakettle. Eldest brother Herb took the photo.

Table of Contents

Foreword

By William D. Middleton

I've known Bob Lewis for quite a few years, but I have to say I didn't know what he was really like until I went with him on one of his railroad trips. The occasion was a two-week journey across a large part of China with a collection of international railroad people and a few railroad enthusiasts back in 1981. Not long after we had left Beijing on a trip to southern China, the whole group gathered for drinks in the lounge car, and after we all had a drink or two, Bob stood on his head, just like he always does on a trip. After a week or so of travel, we finally arrived at Kunming, in southern Yunnan Province. Up until then, we had toured the rolling stock, shops, and lines of China's big main line railroads, but now it was time for something else.

Bob knew about a little meter gauge Indochina-Yunnan railway that could take us all the way south to Hanoi if we wanted, and had managed to schedule a trip over the line for us. Fortunately, I guess, we stopped short of the Vietnam frontier and halted instead at a small town somewhere in southern Yunnan. We unloaded from the train and Bob led us down the street to tour a small enginehouse. The local population clearly had no idea why this strange group of foreigners was there, and did the only thing they could think of, which was to line up along the street and applaud the visitors on their way to the enginehouse.

Train trips with Bob Lewis were like that.

Bob had been running train trips and taking trips to far-off railroads for all of his life. He lived in Pennsylvania for many years, and among the earliest was a series of trips that began in the early 1930s to explore the street railways of

Top: Robert G. Lewis (left) and William D. Middleton have been colleagues and friends for many years. Middleton has been a contributing editor to railroad industry trade magazine Railway Age for a long time; Lewis retired as the magazine's publisher in 1995. Their most recent rail excursion together was Railway Age's *Sesquicentennial Limited* in June 2006, which marked the magazine's 150th year of publishing. Bottom: Lewis and Railway Age Editor-in-Chief William C. Vantuono, who co-authored this book, pose with restored ex-Pennsylvania Railroad E8 5809 at New Jersey Transit's Hoboken Terminal following the *Sesquicentennial Limited's* round-trip run to Bay Head, N.J. 5809 and sister E8 5711, both owned by Bennett Levin's Juniata Terminal Company, powered the train. Photos by Joseph M. Calisi.

Top: Bob Lewis maintains an extensive collection of his own railway photography and memorabilia in his Florida residence. Bottom: At age 93, he can still stand on his head upon request!

Pennsylvania. At that time you couldn't have found a more diverse collection of trolley lines anywhere in the country, and Bob Lewis found just about all of them.

According to Bob's studies, Pennsylvania at that time had more electric railways—roughly 40 in 1934—than any other state, and they offered what must have been a greater variety of operations than just about any other. By far the largest was Philadelphia Rapid Transit, which in 1934 operated 2,914 street cars on a 581-mile system. Pennsylvania's smallest must have been the impressively named Huntingdon, Lewistown & Juniata Valley line, which never got out of Huntingdon and ran four Birney cars on a 1.75-mile right-of-way. Not much longer was the Jersey Shore & Antes Fort Railroad, which was just 2.75 miles long, but crossed the Susquehanna River to run between two states (Pennsylvania and New Jersey). The longest would have been the Philadelphia & Western, which was originally planned as part of a George Gould transcontinental, although P&W settled for its 13.5-mile main line to Norristown.

Pennsylvania must have had more lines named for cities that you never heard of than any other, such as the Skippack & Perkiomen, Hanover & McSherrystown, or Sunbury & Selinsgrove. Many lines were built to "Pennsylvania Trolley Gauge" (5 feet, 2-1/4 or 2-1/2 inches) while other lines used standard gauge. Philadelphia used both. Two Pennsylvania interurban lines used some of the most advanced high speed electric cars ever built, Philadelphia & Western's famous Brill Bullets, and Lehigh Valley Transit's 1930 high speed cars originally built for the Cincinnati & Lake Erie and the Indiana Railroad. Much more common, however, were the aging "first generation" trolleys that kept many of the little lines going until the end, or the popular four-wheel Birney cars that so many lines operated.

Bob Lewis has captured all of this and much more in his journeys in Keystone State Traction. You're sure to learn something about the unusual or unbelievable electric railways of Pennsylvania and many other North American locations that you'd never heard about before.

—*William D. Middleton*

William D. Middleton, the "dean" of electric traction authors, has published over 600 articles for magazines and newspapers around the world and more than 25 books on railroad and electric traction. The Interurban Era *(1961),* The Time of the Trolley *(1967), and* When the Steam Railroads Electrified *(1974) are perhaps his best known. From* Bullets to BART *was his first book for CERA,* The Last Interurbans *was his second. His next one will be, together with his son Bill III, a biography:* Frank Julian Sprague: He Put Electricity Into Transportation, *due out in 2009. Middleton was co-editor with George M. Smerk and Roberta Diehl on the* Encyclopedia of North American Railroads. *Born in Davenport, Iowa, the grandson of the first chief surgeon of the Rock Island Lines, Middleton is a 1950 engineering graduate of Rensselaer Polytechnic Institute and did graduate work in engineering and journalism at the University of Wisconsin. As an officer in the U.S. Navy, he served in a variety of Navy engineering assignments in Turkey, Morocco, the Pacific, and the mainland U.S. Upon retiring from the Navy in 1979, he joined the University of Virginia as its chief facilities officer. He retired again in 1993 and today lives in Charlottesville, Va.*

Introduction

Keystone State Traction was conceived because its principal author, Robert G. Lewis, much better known as "Bob" and approaching his 90th birthday, thought it was a shame to have so much early traction photography languishing, unpublished, in file drawers. He felt that at least the best of his extensive collection ought to be available to today's enthusiasts. This book seemed like a good answer.

During the Great Depression years starting in late 1929, many interurban and local rail transit lines were converting to buses, and rail operations were being abandoned at an appalling rate. However, in 1934, McGraw-Hill's Transit Directory still reported 310 street railway and interurban lines in operation in the United States. Of those 310, the state of Pennsylvania had the most—

Bob Lewis enlisted in the United States Navy on Dec. 8, 1941, the day after Pearl Harbor was attacked. He was stationed in Hawaii. Here is Chief Petty Officer Lewis in August 1945, outside the Oahu Railway's Honolulu enginehouse with Alco 2-8-2 no. 70, which was identical to Denver & Rio Grand Western's Class K28.

38 (Ohio was in second place with 28). Pennsylvania's systems are featured in this book, though we've added a bonus chapter with material from across North America.

A native of Philadelphia's suburban Mount Airy, Bob Lewis lived on Gowen Avenue as a boy. His family's home was located on land that had been part of the estate of Franklin P. Gowen, "Ruler of the Reading." It was just four blocks from the double-track Route 23 trolley line of the Philadelphia Rapid Transit, better-known as the PRT. Bob's walk home after school "took longer that it should have," he relates, with stops to watch activities on the PRT, the Pennsylvania Railroad, and the Reading Railroad. "A favorite was the fireworks generated by the PRT's rail grinder," he says.

Bob, born Dec. 5, 1916, started his railroad career as a messenger in the Pennsylvania Railroad's general offices at Philadelphia's Broad Street Station in August 1934. He had begun his photography of steam railroads and traction lines at age 13, but his new railroad pass privileges gave him the opportunity to extend his travels well beyond Philadelphia and its suburbs. Work ended at 12 noon on Saturdays, and he was often aboard the 1:10 pm train for traction connections at Lancaster, Harrisburg, Greensburg or Pittsburgh, taking photos, many of which are in Keystone State Traction.

Bob and nine rail enthusiast friends met at his home in early 1935 to found the Philadelphia Chapter of the National Railway Historical Society, the organization's second chapter and today one of the largest NRHS chapters. Al Pittman, one of the ten, went on to form the Pittman Electrical Development Company, which pioneered development of miniature electric motors for model trains and trolleys.

March 1937 marked the second anniversary of the founding of the NRHS Philadelphia Chapter. The group scheduled a charter trip over the Reading's Downingtown branch, followed by a dinner at the Sylvania Hotel. Bob invited Roy Wright, Managing Editor of railroad industry trade magazine *Railway Age* in New York City, as guest speaker. Wright declined because of a conflict, but sent his associate, William H. Schmidt, Jr. "Schmidt turned out to be not only an outstanding speaker, but an enthusiastic passenger on our special train and on a Birney-car charter over PRT lines the next day," Bob recalls. "Ten years later, Bill called me in Pittsburgh, where I was working as a PRR reconsignment clerk following a tour of duty with the U.S. Navy in World War II. He offered me a job as Associate Editor of *Railway Age*. I accepted, left the PRR, and moved to Chicago."

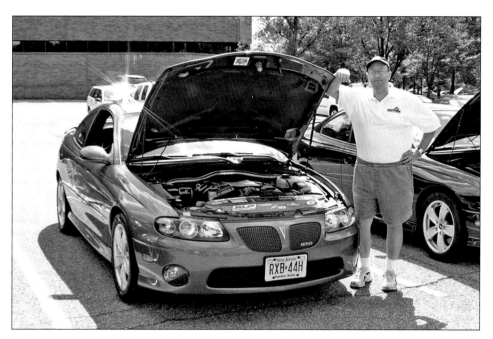

This modified 2004 Pontiac GTO gets Bill Vantuono back and forth from his NJ Transit commuter rail station, "rapid transit" style.

Howard L. Stevens, a retired General Electric engineer, has scratch-built over 100 Connecticut Company revenue and non-revenue trolley models.

In 1950, the Circulation Manager's job opened up in New York at *Railway Age's* publishing company, Simmons-Boardman. Bob was asked to fill it. His business acumen combined with his editorial skills led to his appointment, in 1956, as Publisher of *Railway Age* and the company's other rail magazines, *Railway Track & Structures, Railway Locomotives & Cars,* and *Railway Signaling & Communications.* He was eventually appointed President and Chairman of the Board of Simmons-Boardman.

Bob's first love was steam railroads, but a boyhood friend, William H. Watts, II, who lived just a few blocks away, encouraged him to explore trolley systems. The two would often travel together, cameras at the ready. Bob inherited Watts' traction photo collection when his long-time friend passed on years ago; several of his rarer photos are featured in this book, along with others taken by some of Bob's fellow traction enthusiasts.

Bob semi-retired in 1995 and moved with his wife, Vi, to Ormond By-

The Sea, Florida. He remains active in the industry as a consultant. He also became a member of the Electric Railway Clubs of Florida. It was through this organization that he met co-author Howard L. Stevens, a retired General Electric engineer. Howard, a traction enthusiast and a native of Connecticut, has a vast collection of trolley photographs, some of which are published here, and books. He has scratch-built over 100 Connecticut Company revenue and non-revenue trolley models. In addition to the Electric Railway Clubs of Florida, Howard is a member of the Shore Line Trolley Museum in East Haven, Conn., and a lifetime member of the New Haven Railroad Historical & Technical Association.

Bob and Howard got together, choosing the best photos. Altogether, there are nearly 200 in this book. They enlisted William C. Vantuono, Editor-in-Chief of *Railway Age,* to assemble the photos and text into book form. Bill and Bob and railway industry colleague Robert H. Leilich had collaborated on Bob's first book, Off the Beaten Track (Simmons-Boardman Books, 2004), which featured Bob's steam railroad photography. Bob had hired Bill in 1992 as Assistant Editor of *Railway Age,* having met him on a New Jersey Transit North Jersey Coast Line commuter train in 1991. Bill, whom Bob says "was a natural for the job," was promoted to Managing Editor in 1993, Executive Editor in 1996, and Editor-in-Chief in 2000, succeeding Luther S. Miller, whom Bob had hired in 1958. (Luther became the magazine's Senior Editorial Consultant and to this day remains an integral part of *Railway Age's* editorial staff.)

Bill does plenty of train riding. He lives in Brick, N.J., and drives to Manasquan Station on NJ Transit's North Jersey Coast Line to take the train into New York—a 125-mile round trip each day. Bill has published a railroad book of his own, All About Railroading (Simmons-Boardman Books, 2000, now in its second edition), written especially for young adults and rail industry new-hires. He recently completed editing the fifth edition of John Armstrong's The Railroad: What It Is, What It Does (Simmons-Boardman Books, 2008). Bill's introduction to railways was with PCC cars. As a young boy in Newark N.J., his father would often take him for rides on the Newark City Subway from Branch Brook Park to Newark Penn Station, where they would watch Pennsylvania Railroad and Jersey Central trains pulling in.

Bill is also an automotive and motorsports enthusiast. He is National Chapter Coordinator for the Pontiac GTO Association of America and writes for the association's monthly magazine, *The Legend.* Aside from passenger trains, his preferred mode of travel is his modified 2004 "Goat."

If we didn't treat your favorite trolley line as well as all the others featured in Keystone State Traction, it's only because the author's camera didn't get there, or the weather was bad. Bob's favorites were Lehigh Valley Transit Company and West Penn Railways, but hardly to the exclusion of others. He says he "never met a rail vehicle he wouldn't photograph."

Putting together this book was a lot of work but a lot of fun—truly a labor of love. We hope readers find it truly interesting. Someday, perhaps 50 or 100 years from now, will someone be doing a book like this on modern light rail? And what will have replaced it? Hopefully, nothing!

Robert G. Lewis
Howard L. Stevens
William C. Vantuono

Allentown & Reading Traction Company

Allentown & Reading Traction Co. Birney car no. 8 at its truncated terminal at Dorney Park in early 1936.

A&RTC car No. 2 at County Home, near Wescoesville, July 1, 1934. Photo by William H. Watts, II/Robert G. Lewis collection.

The Allentown & Reading Traction Company never did reach Reading, but at Kutztown, where the company's maintenance facility was located, you could change to the Reading Street Railway Company's (p. 64) "Pennsylvania Broad Gauge" (5 feet 2-1/4 inches) line to Reading. A&RTC was standard gauge, which allowed it to access downtown Allentown over Lehigh Valley Transit (p. 33) trackage. A&RTC service had been cut back to Dorney Park—a 42-minute run out of Allentown—when the photo at left was taken. In March 1936, even this truncated mileage was abandoned.

Altoona & Logan Valley car no. 170 takes the Buena Vista siding on the 14-mile Tyrone line in May 1936. The Pennsylvania Railroad's four-track main line is on the right.

The Altoona & Logan Valley Electric Railway used "Pennsylvania Trolley Gauge" of 5 feet, 2 inches. Cars and track were well-maintained up until service was discontinued on Aug. 7, 1954. Until 1937, when the Tyrone line was abandoned due to severe flood damage in March of that year, there were 54 miles of line, and almost 100 cars in service. Outside of Altoona, much of the line was on private rights-of-way, or side-of-road. The car barn and shops were at Eldorado, three and a half miles south of Altoona on the 7-1/2-mile, double-track Hollidaysburg line.

Buses replaced electric railway service. In 1959, the A&LV became the publicly owned Altoona & Logan Valley Bus Authority. Interurban bus service outside the Bus Authority's territory reached Hollidaysburg by Blue & White Bus Lines, and Tyrone by Fullington Auto Bus Co.. Both of these services operated into the 1970s. Altoona Metro Transit (Amtran) replaced the Altoona & Logan Valley Bus Authority in 1977. Amtran currently serves Hollidaysburg.

Seven cents, a bargain even in 1936, to ride the railway. Today, a one-way adult bus ticket on Altoona Metro Transit is $1.35—still a bargain.

A&LVER car no. 73, built by Osgood Bradley in 1929, en route on the double-track Hollidaysburg line to Eldorado, site of the railway's car barn and shops.

Conestoga Traction Company

June 20, 1937: No. 67, one of Conestoga's Cincinnati-built cars on charter to the National Railway Historical Society, poses on a bridge across Conestoga Creek, on the Ephrata line. The bridge looks like it might have been built to handle the PRR's *Broadway Limited* on a detour rather than Conestoga's lightweight cars.

At its peak, Conestoga Traction Company operated an extensive network of lines centered in Lancaster, its headquarters city. In 1934, it had on its roster 71 steel motor cars purchased from Cincinnati Car Company in 1924, and operated 130 miles of line. Seven city routes—one a loop line serving the Pennsylvania Railroad station—were complemented by lines that "boxed the compass," running roughly northeast to Ephrata, east to Coatesville, southwest to Columbia, and west to Elizabethtown.

Through connections to adjacent interurban companies such as the Philadelphia & West Chester (later Red Arrow and now SEPTA Route 101), West Chester Street Railway, Schuylkill Valley Traction, Reading Transit, Hershey Transit, and Harrisburg Railways, it was possible to ride trolleys—slowly and circuitously—from Philadelphia to Harrisburg. There were two choices: a southern route via West Chester-Coatesville-Lancaster-Hershey, and a northern route via Norristown-Pottstown-Reading-Ephrata-Lebanon-Hershey.

Conestoga Traction was also a freight hauler, transporting milk and produce from area farms into town. Most famously, through its connection with Hershey Transit, it transported milk to the Hershey Chocolate Company for chocolate production.

Though Conestoga Traction had abandoned many of its lines by 1932, rail service survived until September 1947, when Conestoga's last trolleys—a Lancaster city operation—made their final runs.

	DAY	8	1_	24
	1	9	17	25
	2	10	18	26
	3	11	19	27
	4	12	20	28
	5	13	21	29
	6	14	22	30
	7	15	23	31

CON STOG.. TRACTION CO.
SUNDAY - PASS
75c **75c**

Price .... Price

This pass is good for unlimited rides on all cars of this company on date as punched for the passenger to whom it was originally sold. This pass is to remain in the passenger's possession during the entire time subject to inspection by conductor.

VOID IF TRANSFERRED OR RESOLD

GEN. MGR.

1927	1928	1929	1930		
JAN.	FEB.	MAR.	APR.	MAY	JUN.
JUL.	AUG.	SEP.	OCT.	NOV.	DEC.

Conestoga Traction Company's Sunday Pass sold for 75 cents in 1930. It was good on all cars and all lines for unlimited rides on the date of sale.

Nine years later, on an early March day in 1946, another NRHS charter car traverses the Ephrata line.

Howard E. Johnston was also on the June 1937 NRHS special. He shot this scene of no. 67 near Brownstown, Lancaster County. William D. Middleton collection.

Here's no. 67 in regular service, eastbound at the Reading Company crossing on 4th Street in Columbia. The date is Sept. 27, 1937. James P. Shuman photo/William D. Middleton collection.

13

Conestoga Traction Company

May 1934: Open-bench car 174 at Maple Grove station, the end of a short branch line that served Rocky Springs Amusement Park.

Car 60, left, and car 59 meet at Ginover turnout on Conestoga's Lancaster-Coatesville line, July 3, 1932. Photo by John J. Bowman/Robert G. Lewis collection.

NEFFSVILLE JUNIOR HIGH SCHOOL

CAR TICKET

Name *Robert Witmer*

is a student of this school and entitled to transportation

School year of 19 29 19 30

Signed *A. N. Gingrich*

Principal

Stock Yards

Conestoga Traction also issued student passes. This one was issued for the 1929-1930 school year to Robert Witmer, who attended Neffsville Junior High School. Robert G. Lewis collection.

Fairmount Park Transit Company

No. 10, one of the ten big closed cars that ran in the winter when Woodside Park was closed, is at its northeast terminal at 33rd and Dauphin, where it connected with cars of the Philadelphia Rapid Transit. No. 10 was built by Brill in 1896. This car was the last one to operate, since it was used to power the work cars for the line's dismantling, which was completed in early 1947. This scene is from the winter of 1935.

A one-of-a-kind, the Fairmount Park Transit Company seems to have been hidden from the press, perhaps by the heavy shade of the trees that lined its tracks winding through Philadelphia's great Fairmount Park.

Built in 1896 primarily to provide transportation to Woodside Park, a large amusement park near the center of Fairmount Park not served by public roads, the line became an attraction in itself with its 8.8-mile scenic route and its open bench cars and trailers. It also served a year-round function even after the park closed for the winter as a shortcut for passengers from Philadelphia's northeast to its southeast across the Schuylkill River.

A roster of just ten closed cars was supplemented by 50 open bench cars—20 of which were motorized—during the summer months. The accompanying map (p. 16) shows how the line started from a loop station, crossed the river on a high double-track bridge, and wound through the park. Only the condemning of this bridge in 1946, and the lack of resources to replace it, led to the closing and scrapping of this unique line. Had the failure of the bridge not taken place, it is possible that the abandonment would not have occurred. Certainly, low patronage was not a factor: On the Fourth of July prior to the closure, its conductors rang up more than 37,000 fares!

Up to the day of its closing, Sept. 9, 1946, the line was running full schedules over its 15.22 miles of track. The line was sold to a scrap dealer for $50,000 and was promptly dismantled.

An interesting footnote: The author's good friend, Al Pittman, founder of the Pittman Electrical Development Co., pioneer manufacturer of small electric motors for model trains and trolleys, worked as a conductor on Fairmount Park's open cars during summer vacations from Rensselaer Polytechnic Institute.

Fairmount Park Transit Company

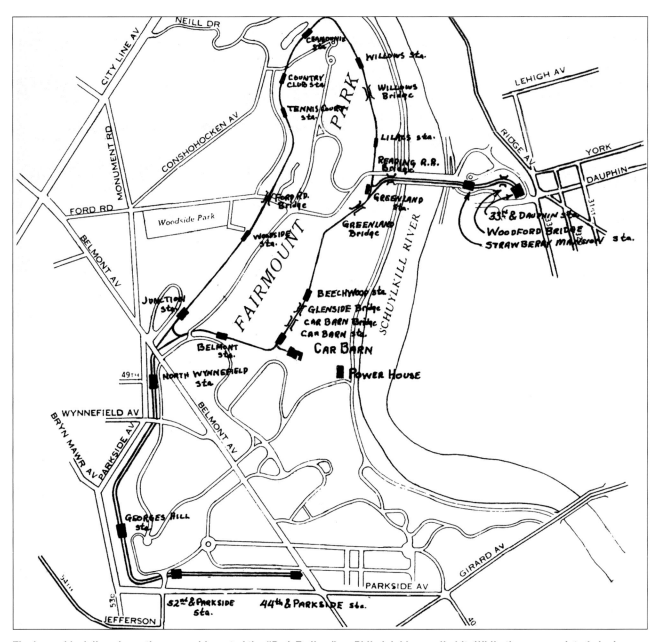

The heavy black line shows the unusual layout of the "Park Trolley," as Philadelphians called it. While there was a lot of single track, the return loop served, in effect, as a second track.

Two-car trains were common for summertime operations. Here, car no. 25 and trailer no. 39 are at the Strawberry Mansion stop on Sept. 2, 1934. William H. Watts, II photo/Robert G. Lewis collection.

Hanover & McSherrystown Street Railway

Brill Double Truck Convertible car no. 100 at Hanover Square, September 1928. William H. Watts, II photo/Robert G. Lewis collection.

The Hanover & McSherrystown Street Railway had a single 11.6-mile line linking those two towns and connecting with York Railways at Hanover. It opened in 1906. In 1922, the General Gas & Electric Co. acquired the railway. There were 14 Brill Double Truck Convertible passenger cars and three work cars servicing the line as of 1927. Service was discontinued in 1931 and the line was promptly torn up

Interior of Double Truck Convertible car showing smoking compartment for 20 people, at rear. Total seating capacity was 44 people. Notice the cane covered seats. Brill photo, 1908.

Harrisburg Railways Company

Harrisburg Railways car no. 70 crossing the broad Swatara Creek en route to Hummelstown, November 1936. The Middletown line crossed the same stream a few miles to the north. Further upstream, Conestoga Traction crossed the Swatara, too.

Car no. 801 at the end of the Rockville line, November 1936.

HARRISBURG RAILWAYS COMPANY
EMPLOYE'S TICKET One 7-cent Fare
If person presenting same displays badge on outer garments. Not good for Ladies or Children.

Badge No.

Name

F. B. MUSSER, Pres't

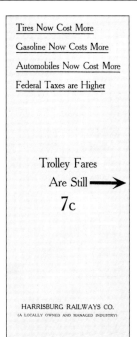

Tires Now Cost More

Gasoline Now Costs More

Automobiles Now Cost More

Federal Taxes are Higher

Trolley Fares
Are Still ⟶
7c

HARRISBURG RAILWAYS CO.
(A LOCALLY OWNED AND MANAGED INDUSTRY)

What was true in '32 is still (except for 7 cent fares) valid today. The back cover of this July 3, 1932 timetable compared the per-trip cost of driving to that of taking Harrisburg Railways. "Save money for your automobile vacation by using the trolley cars for business—and you will have fewer accidents and repair bills," it proclaimed.

Public transportation in Harrisburg started in 1865 with a horse-drawn trolley. Harrisburg City Passenger Railway Company acquired this operation in 1873 and began to expand it. The East Harrisburg Passenger Railway was formed in 1886 to provide service in the city's Allison Hill and then Steelton sections, on the east side of the Susquehanna River. The latter company tested the city's first electric trolley on July 4, 1888, and started electrified service on both lines two weeks later. Harrisburg City Railway began electrification in early 1891, and in April of that year, the two companies merged under the East Harrisburg name. The following year, another company, the Citizens Passenger Railway Company, formed to provide service to the Steelton and Oberlin areas, with extensions into Harrisburg. The Citizens and East Harrisburg companies merged in 1895 to form the Harrisburg Traction Company. In 1903, Harrisburg Traction expanded service to Linglestown, Hummelstown and Dauphin, and changed its name to the Central Pennsylvania Traction Company. Ten years later, a reorganization occurred to form the Harrisburg Railways Company.

Harrisburg Railways, as of 1931, operated 74.6 miles of track. Lines radiated to Middletown, Hummelstown, Linglestown, Rockville, and Oberlin. Harrisburg Railway's cars connected with those of Valley Railways (p. 80) in downtown Harrisburg, and with those of Hershey Transit (p. 20) at Hummelstown. Total car ownership in 1934 was 99, plus 10 work cars. On July 16, 1939, all rail operations ended, and were converted to buses, though the company retained its "Railways" name. In 1973, the City of Harrisburg and Dauphin and Cumberland counties formed a public authority to acquire Harrisburg Railways and Valley Railways successor Valley Transit to form Capital Area Transit.

Hershey Transit

Dec. 30, 1934: Hershey Transit car no. 27, on the broad loop at the end of the Hotel Hershey line, is heading back downtown.

Hershey Transit was part of the extensive Hershey Chocolate Company. Many of the transit line's passengers were people who worked at the chocolate factory. Milk cars ran daily, collecting milk in cans from local farms along its lines. A short line west from Hershey to Hummelstown connected with Harrisburg Railways (p. 19). Another line ran southwest to Elizabethtown. Two easterly lines ran to Palmyra and Lebanon. A short loop line ran up a steep grade to serve the grand Hotel Hershey. The company's car and track were well-maintained right up to the day service ended in 1946.

Car no. 30 was bought from Grand Rapids, Mich., in 1936, to service the Hotel Hershey line. It was sold, in 1942, to Marion, Ind. No. 21 is in the rear. Howard L. Stevens collection.

TIME-TABLE
OF THE
HERSHEY TRANSIT COMPANY
HERSHEY, PENNSYLVANIA

Hummelstown - Hershey -
Palmyra Division

Hotel Hershey - Hershey -
Campbelltown Division

EFFECTIVE NOV. 1, 1942

The time shown in this folder is Eastern War Time.

Hotel Hershey - Hershey - Campbelltown

EAST BOUND			WEST BOUND		
LEAVE HOTEL HERSHEY	LEAVE HERSHEY	ARRIVE CAMPB'T'N	LEAVE CAMPB'T'N	LEAVE HERSHEY	ARRIVE HOTEL HERSHEY
	†5 15	†5 45	†5 30	†5 45	
	†5 45	†6 15	†6 15	†6 30	6 45
	‡6 30	‡6 45	‡6 45	†7 00	7 15
†6 45	†7 00		7 45	8 00	8 15
7 15	7 30	7 45	8 45	9 00	9 15
8 15	8 30	8 45	9 45	10 00	10 15
9 15	9 30	9 45	10 45	11 00	11 15
10 15	10 30	10 45	11 45	12 00	12 15
11 15	11 30	11 45	12 45	1 00	1 15
12 15	12 30	12 45	1 45	2 00	2 15
1 15	1 30	1 45	2 45	3 00	3 15
2 15	2 30	2 45	3 45	4 00	4 15
3 15	3 30	3 45	4 45	5 00	5 15
4 15	4 30	4 45	5 45	6 00	6 15
5 15	5 30	5 45	6 45	7 00	7 15
6 15	6 30	6 45	7 45	8 00	8 15
7 15	7 30	7 45	8 45	9 00	9 15
8 15	8 30	8 45	9 45	10 00	10 15
9 15	9 30	9 45	10 45	11 00	11 15
10 15	10 30	10 45	11 45	12 00	12 15
11 15	11 30	11 45			
12 15	12 30				

A.M. time indicated by light face figures.
P.M. time indicated by black face figures.
† Daily, except Sunday and holidays.
‡ First car on Sunday.

HERSHEY PARK
"The Summer Playground of Pennsylvania" has all outdoor amusements

Four Golf Courses—54 Holes
Picnic Grounds of 1,000 Acres
Orchestras of National Reputation
Play Dance Music in the Ballroom
GOLF--April to mid-November;
BALLROOM and PARK--
May to Labor Day

Hummelstown - Hershey - Palmyra

EAST BOUND			WEST BOUND		
LEAVE HUM'ST'N	LEAVE HERSHEY	ARRIVE PALMYRA	LEAVE PALMYRA	LEAVE HERSHEY	ARRIVE HUM'ST'N
	†5 15	†5 30	†5 30	†6 00	†6 15
†5 30	†5 45	†6 00		‡6 15	‡6 30
‡6 15	‡6 00	‡6 15	6 45	7 00	7 15
6 15	6 30	6 45	6 45	7 00	7 15
6 45	7 00	7 15	7 15	7 30	7 45
7 15	7 30	7 45	7 45	8 00	8 15
7 45	8 00	8 15	8 15	8 30	8 45
8 15	8 30	8 45	8 45	9 00	9 15
8 45	9 00	9 15	9 15	9 30	9 45
9 15	9 30	9 45	9 45	10 00	10 15
9 45	10 00	10 15	10 15	10 30	10 45
10 15	10 30	10 45	10 45	11 00	11 15
10 45	11 00	11 15	11 15	11 30	11 45
11 15	11 30	:11 45	11 45	12 00	12 15
11 45	12 00	12 15	12 15	12 30	12 45
12 15	12 30	12 45	12 45	1 00	1 15
12 45	1 00	1 15	1 15	1 30	1 45
1 15	1 30	1 45	1 45	2 00	2 15
1 45	2 00	2 15	2 15	2 30	2 45
2 15	2 30	2 45	2 45	3 00	3 15
2 45	3 00	3 15	3 15	3 30	3 45
3 15	3 30	3 45	3 45	4 00	4 15
3 45	4 00	4 15	4 15	4 30	4 45
4 15	4 30	4 45	4 45	5 00	5 15
4 45	5 00	5 15	5 15	5 30	5 45
5 15	5 30	5 45	5 45	6 00	6 15
5 45	6 00	6 15	6 15	6 30	6 45
6 15	6 30	6 45	6 45	7 00	7 15
6 45	7 00	7 15	7 15	7 30	7 45
7 15	7 30	7 45	7 45	8 00	8 15
7 45	8 00	8 15	8 15	8 30	8 45
8 15	8 30	8 45	8 45	9 00	9 15
8 45	9 00	9 15	9 15	9 30	9 45
9 15	9 30	9 45	9 45	10 00	10 15
9 45	10 00	10 15	10 15	10 30	10 45
10 15	10 30	10 45	10 45	11 00	11 15
10 45	11 00	11 15	11 15	11 30	11 45
11 15	11 30	11 45	11 45	12 00	12 15
11 45	12 00	12 15	12 15	12 30	
12 15	12 30				

A.M. time in light face figures. P.M. black face.
† Daily except Sunday and holidays.
‡ First car on Sundays.
West bound cars leaving Hershey on the half hour connect with Harrisburg bus at Hummelstown. East bound, leaving Hershey on the hour, connects at Palmyra for Annville, Cleona and Lebanon.
Daily except Saturday P.M. and Sunday, 15 minute service Hershey to Palmyra, 5:15 to 8:15 A.M., and 3:00 to 6:00 P.M.

Hershey Transit's 1942 wartime schedule for its Palmayra and Campellstown lines. Howard L. Stevens collection.

Oct. 6, 1934: Car no. 20 at the end of its run in Elizabethtown, having delivered the morning newspapers, stacked outside the front door.

Hershey Transit

Four photos by C.L. Siebert, Jr. (William D. Middleton collection) from the late 1930s. Clockwise from top left: Hershey Transit no. 2 on an Aug. 13, 1939 NRHS fan trip crosses a trestle over the Pennsylvania Railroad's Conewago & Lebanon Branch at Beverly. On May 6, 1938, no. 17 is seen arriving from Elizabethtown at the junction of the Lebabon and Elizabethtown lines on U.S. Route 322. Back to Aug. 13, 1939: On the same NRHS fan trip, no. 2 is at Shank's Church in Elizabethtown. This car,

and sisters 1-3, were not used in scheduled service in later years. However, on Sunday mornings, each was used without fail to bring the boys from the Milton S. Hershey trade school to Sunday school. On that same August day, nos. 7 and 30 are paused at the Hotel Hershey. No. 7 is a scheduled-service car; no. 30 is on a fan trip. No. 7 is a former Lancaster, Ephrata & Lebanon Street Railway (p. 30) car; no. 30 had been acquired from Grand Rapids and was later sold to Marion, Ind. The famous, luxurious Hotel Hershey is at left.

Huntingdon, Lewistown & Juniata Valley

One of Huntingdon's four Birney cars in the center of Route 30, the Lincoln Highway, September 1930. William H. Watts, II, photo/Robert G. Lewis collection.

The Huntingdon, Lewistown & Juniata Valley never got off the streets of Huntingdon. As chartered, it would have gone east to Belleville, paralleled the Kishacoquillas Valley Railroad to Burnham, and paralleled or taken over the Lewistown & Reedsville Electric Railway (p. 40) to Lewistown. Its ambitious plans were never fulfilled, but its four Birney cars did run along 1.75 miles of single track until service was terminated in 1930.

Jersey Shore & Antes Fort Railroad

Car no. 3 on the temporary bridge in a 1907 photograph. Nathan Zapler collection, photographer unknown.

The Jersey Shore & Antes Fort Railroad operated 2.75 miles of line from Jersey Shore across the Susquehanna River to Antes Fort, where it connected with the Pennsylvania Railroad, and—for freight only—2.25 miles from Jersey Shore to Nippano. The line had three interurban combine cars, built by Niles Car and Manufacturing Company in 1906. According to the 1908 Official Guide, freight service was operated by steam, but no record of steam equipment is available. (Hopefully, steam locomotives did not operate on the temporary bridge shown in the photo above.) The Jersey Shore was abandoned in 1925. Car no. 3 is now at the Pennsylvania Trolley Museum in Washington, Pa.. The museum describes its unusual preservation history:

"When the company folded, its owners took the cars to a site along nearby Pine Creek and fashioned a residence from them. Thus saved from the scrapper, the cars sat until June 1972, when Hurricane Agnes brought extensive flooding to the area. Down Pine Creek they floated, coming to rest near a railroad bridge, which badly damaged them. Discovered by Jeff Pritchard, who worked on the body and saved it from destruction, and later moved it to the facilities of Paul Vassallo, no. 3 survived. Vassallo made the car available to the Pennsylvania Trolley Museum in 1999."

Car no. 3 at Jersey Shore, followed by a work train led by car no. 2. Nathan Zapler collection, photographer unknown. Photo courtesy of the Pennsylvania Trolley Museum.

Johnstown Traction Company

Johnstown Traction Company car no. 230 at Ferndale, May 18, 1940.

The Johnstown Traction Company was formed in 1910. In 1934, it operated 41.8 miles of line and had 77 cars on its roster. In May 1940, when the photo of car no. 230 was taken at Ferndale, there were still six routes in service. On June 11, 1960, all streetcar service ended, making Johnstown one of the last small cities to abandon trolley service in the United States. Electric trolleybus service, which began in 1951 on one route, continued until 1967, after which the system became bus-only. In 1976, the privately owned company became the CamTran public transit system.

At least nine Johnstown cars survive. No. 358 went to Stone Mountain, Ga., where it was converted to diesel power; it then went to a museum at Kingston, N.Y., where it was restored. Cars 311 and 353 went to the Trolley Museum of Pennsylvania at Orbisonia. The 356 and 357 went to the Shoreline Museum at Branford, Conn.; the 350 to the Pennsylvania Trolley Museum at Washington, Pa.; the 351 to the Market Street Railway in San Francisco, Calif.; the 352 to the National Capitol Trolley Museum in Silver Spring, Md.; and the 362 to the Fox River Trolley Museum in South Elgin, Ill. Surely no other traction line has so many cars preserved in so many repositories.

Car no. 314 is one of a group of seven acquired from the Connecticut Company Hartford Division in 1942. Photographer unknown/Howard L. Stevens collection.

PCC car 411 on the Coopersdale line, October 1950. The 411 was one of 17 new PCC cars ordered in 1945 from St. Louis Car and placed in service beginning in January 1947. They were the first "all electric" St. Louis cars, and Johnstown was the smallest city in the United States to operate them.

Car no. 249, one of five cars built by Brill in 1901 and numbered 247-251, at Dale in 1939. Notice the Galliker's Ice Cream truck in the background? Galliker's is still producing premium ice cream today, as well as other products. Located in Johnstown, Galliker's has been in business for almost 100 years. It's a fourth-generation, family owned company, with approximately 350 employees in two processing plants and eleven distribution centers. It's known as "the region's top ice cream company." So, even though you can't savor a trolley ride anymore in Johnstown, you can still savor delicious Galliker's ice cream! Photographer unknown/Howard L. Stevens collection.

Lackawanna & Wyoming Valley

High speeds were possible on the Laurel Line's double-tracked, block-signaled, crossing-free line. One of its steel cars, built by Osgood Bradley in 1925, heads toward Wilkes-Barre on a cold day in March, 1939. D.H. Cope photo/Robert G. Lewis collection.

Railroad

The Lackawanna & Wyoming Valley Railroad, best known as "The Laurel Line," was built more to steam railroad standards than most traction lines. It opened its 29-mile double-track, third-rail-powered line between Wilkes-Barre and Scranton in 1895. The railway was protected by automatic block signals, and—a claim few other transit lines could make—had, outside its street level entry into Wilkes-Barre where overhead catenary was required—no highway crossings at grade.

Its entry into Scranton was on a 4% grade, but in 1907 the grade was bypassed, replaced by a single-track tunnel just short of one mile in length. That part of the original line became its Dunmore branch.

Freight was an important part of the Laurel Line's traffic, and cars were interchanged with all the Class I railroads serving the area. Three Baldwin-Westinghouse electric locomotives, the first built in 1895, served The Laurel Line until it closed on Dec. 31, 1952.

Locomotive No. 403 is at Pittston with a three-car freight in 1951. Bill Slade photo/Robert G. Lewis collection.

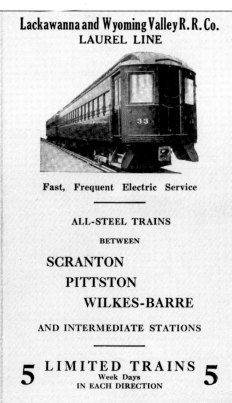

Lackawanna and Wyoming Valley R. R. Co.
LAUREL LINE

Fast, Frequent Electric Service

ALL-STEEL TRAINS

BETWEEN

SCRANTON
PITTSTON
WILKES-BARRE

AND INTERMEDIATE STATIONS

5 LIMITED TRAINS 5
Week Days
IN EACH DIRECTION

FAST PACKAGE EXPRESS
IN BAGGAGE CARS
20—TRAINS DAILY—20
(Including Sundays and Holidays)

45—Minutes Between Terminals—45

This service operates between Agency Stations only, namely: Scranton, Pittston, Plains and Wilkes-Barre. It is a station to station service and packages must be delivered to and taken from Baggage Rooms.

RATES (Charges must be prepaid)

Weight	Amount	Weight	Amount
0– 5 lbs	$0.30	51– 60 lbs	$0.80
6–10 "	.35	61– 70 "	.85
11–15 "	.40	71– 80 "	.90
16–20 "	.45	81– 90 "	.95
21–25 "	.50	91–100 "	1.00
26–30 "	.55	101–125 "	1.10
31–35 "	.60	126–150 "	1.20
36–40 "	.65	151–175 "	1.30
41–45 "	.70	176–200 "	1.40
46–50 "	.75		

Rates are for single packages.
Maximum weight 200 pounds.

ACCIDENT INSURANCE
ON SALE AT TICKET OFFICES
25c. INSURES FOR $5000

This Nov. 16, 1928 timetable features the Lackawanna & Wyoming Valley's express package rates. Imagine shipping a 200-pound package for $1.65, including insurance! Robert G. Lewis collection.

Lancaster, Ephrata & Lebanon Street Railway

Lancaster, Ephrata & Lebanon car No. 20 at Ephrata, July 8, 1928. William H. Watts, II, photo/Robert G. Lewis collection.

The Lancaster, Ephrata & Lebanon Street Railway built its single-track line between the two towns in its name in 1914. Just 17 years later, in May 1931, the railway was abandoned. Its 23-mile line connected with Conestoga Transit at Ephrata, and with Hershey Transit at Lebanon; it didn't serve any large towns. The LE&LSR had three state-of-the art cars built by Cincinnati Car Co. in 1914. Two were sold to Hershey Transit, which renumbered them nos. 4 and 7.

LANCASTER, EPHRATA & LEBANON STREET RAILWAY COMPANY
WINTER TIME TABLE
(SOUTHBOUND)
Lebanon to Schaefferstown and Ephrata
EFFECTIVE SEPTEMBER 1st, 1928

LEBANON	REISTVILLE	SCHAEFFERS-TOWN	KLEINFELTERS-VILLE	SOUTH MOUNTAIN	HOPELAND	CLAY	LINCOLN	EPHRATA
AM	AM	AM	AM	AM	AM	AM	AM	AM
$5.90	$6.24	$5.31	$5.38	$5.45	$5.52	$5.58	$6.05	$6.15
$6.30	$6.54	$7.01	$7.08	$7.15	$7.22	$7.26	$7.35	$7.45
8.30	8.54	9.01	9.08	9.15	9.22	9.26	9.35	9.45
10.00	10.24	10.31	10.38	10.45	10.52	10.56	11.06	11.15
11.30	11.54	12.01	12.08	12.15	12.22	12.26	12.35	12.45
1.00	1.24	1.31	1.38	1.45	1.52	1.56	2.05	2.15
2.30	2.54	3.01	3.08	3.15	3.22	3.26	3.35	3.45
4.00	4.24	4.31	4.38	4.45	4.52	4.56	5.03	5.15
5.30	5.54	6.01	6.08	6.15	6.22	6.26	6.35	6.45
7.00	7.24	7.31	7.38	7.45	7.52	7.56	8.48	8.15
*8.30	*8.54	*9.01	*9.08	*9.35	*9.22	*9.26	*9.35	*9.45
$9.00	$9.24	$9.31	$9.38	$9.45	$9.52	$9.56	$10.05	$10.15
*10.30	*10.54	*11.01	*11.08	*11.15	*11.22	*11.26	*11.35	*11.45
s10.45	s11.09	s11.16	s11.23	s11.30	s11.37	s11.41	s11.50	s12.00

P.M. indicated by heavy faced type.
‡ Does not run Sundays.
§ First car Sundays.
* Does not run Saturdays nor Sundays.
s Runs Saturdays and Sundays only.

SHIP BY TROLLEY EXPRESS
(Express Service at Freight Rates)
WEEK DAYS EXPRESS CAR
Leaves Ephrata for Lebanon for intermediate points at 6:15 A.M. and 10 A.M.
Leaves Lebanon for Ephrata for intermediate points at 8:30 A.M. and 1 P.M.
Schedule of Trains given herein are subject to change without notice. Time shown is that at which this Company will endeavor to have Cars arrive at and depart from Stations, but the time of arrival and departure is not guaranteed. Time at Junction Points shown for convenient reference should not be considered as assurance that connections will be made. This Company can not and does not guarantee connections, and will not be responsible for delays ensuing therefrom.
Passenger Parcel Service is cheap and convenient.
Saves YOUR time and money.
Express Service is prompt and reliable in all kinds of weather.
Inquire at Office.

Southbound LE&LSR timetable for the winter of 1928.

Lancaster & York Furnace Street Railway

Lancaster & York Furnace car no. 4 at Millersville, Sept. 27, 1927. Photographer unknown/Robert G. Lewis collection.

T he Lancaster & York Furnace Street Railway Co. operated just over 12 miles of line, all on private right-of-way, between Quarryville and Millersville, where it connected with Conestoga Traction's (p. 12) line to Lancaster. The line opened in 1903 and was abandoned on Oct. 15, 1930.

SCHEDULE
Lancaster and York Furnace St. Ry. Co.
Effective July 1, 1920

LEAVE MILLERSVILLE	LEAVE PEQUEA
6.00 A. M.	
8.00	7.00 A. M.
9.30	8.45
11.30	10.30
1.30 P. M.	12.30 P. M.
3.30	2.30
6.00	5.10
*7.30	6.45

Saturdays Cars Leave Millersville at
6, 7, 8, 9, 10, 11, 12 A. M.
1, 2, 3:30, 4, 5, 6, *7, 8, 9:30, *11:30 P. M.

Sundays Cars Leave Millersville at
7:30, 8:30, 9:30, 10:30, 11:30 A. M.
12:30, 1:30, 2:30, 3:30, 4:30, 5:30, 6:30,
7:30, *8:30, *9:30 P. M.

Saturdays Cars Leave Pequea at
7, 8, 9, 10, 11, 12 A. M.
1, 2, 3, 4, 5, 6, 7, 8:45, 10:40 P. M.

Sundays Cars Leave Pequea at
8:30, 9:30, 10:30, 11:30 A. M.
12:30, 1:30, 2:30, 3:30, 4:30, 5:30, 6:30
7:30, 8:30 P. M.

*To Marticville Car Barn

L&YFSR timetable for summer 1920.

Lehigh Traction Company

Lehigh Traction car 60, photographed in downtown Hazelton in June 1929. This scene is easily dated by the automobile at right. The no. 60's lone center door made it almost necessary for a second man to collect fares. William H. Watts, II photo/Robert G. Lewis collection.

The Lehigh Traction Company operated about 10 miles of street railways in Hazelton and adjoining communities. There were 25 passenger cars and five service cars on the roster when trolley service was withdrawn in 1932.

This 1912 car barn postcard makes Lehigh traction look like a double-track main line railroad, especially when contrasted with the local road on its left. Robert G. Lewis collection.

Lehigh Valley Transit Company

LVT No. 1020 on the left and 1002 on the right, both former Cincinnati & Lake Erie cars, are at 8th & Hamilton Streets in Allentown, terminal station for the Liberty Bell Limiteds, Feb. 19, 1939.

The Lehigh Valley Transit Company operated an extensive network of streetcar lines and interurban services centered on its headquarters city, Allentown. Track-miles, in 1934, totaled 132, and 185 cars were on its roster, not counting 11 freight motors and 45 service cars. Besides local lines serving Allentown, there were local lines in nearby Bethlehem and Easton, and an intercity line connecting the three.

The LVT was most noted for its 42-mile line from Allentown to Norristown, where its limited cars served Coopersburg, Quakertown, Perkasie, Souderton, Lansdale, and Center Square before continuing 13.5 miles over the Philadelphia & Western (p. 50) to 69th Street Terminal in Upper Darby. The LVT proudly called this the "Liberty Bell Route."

The Reading Railroad paralleled much of the LVT's route and operated passenger trains directly into its downtown-Philadelphia's Reading Terminal.

However, for cash-strapped riders, especially during the Great Depression years, the LVT was much less expensive.

In the 1930s, the LVT began modernizing its car fleet through purchases from other lines that had abandoned rail operations, notably nine streamlined cars from the Cincinnati & Lake Erie and one from the Indiana Railroad. These cars took over the hourly express service on the Allentown-Philadelphia route. Six modern cars from the Dayton & Troy railway replaced older cars on the Allentown-Bethlehem-Easton run.

Like most passenger rail services nationwide, the LVT's ridership peaked during World War II, then declined following the war as people returned to their automobiles and the U.S. government ramped up highway construction.

It was a sad day for electric railway enthusiasts when the LVT, which had been gradually replacing trolleys with buses, ran its last car on June 8, 1953.

Lehigh Valley Transit Company

One of the former Cincinnati & Lake Erie cars speeds south out of Sellersville on a summer day in 1946. The plant in the background is the home of the Pittman Electrical Development Company, maker of motors for the model railway trade. Al Pittman, a close friend of Bob Lewis's and a fellow Philadelphian, founded this company. In 1935, he was, with Bob, one of 10 founders of the Philadelphia Chapter of the National Railway Historical Society, the organization's second chapter and today one of the largest NRHS chapters.

LVT cars 803 and 805 running as Works Progress Administration (WPA) specials at NACE Siding, just north of Telford, Aug. 24, 1936. J. Hansell Lewis, Bob's older brother, took this photo. Hansell often accompanied Bob on his excursions.

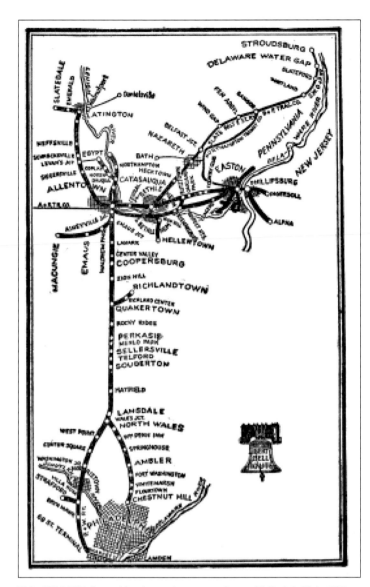

This 1929 LVT timetable shows the connection to Philadelphia's 69th Street Terminal over the Philadelphia & Western (lower left).

Car no. 701 at West Overbrook, operating on the third-rail Philadelphia & Western line, Aug. 23, 1935.

Car no. 177 in local service at West Point, between Lansdale and Norristown, on a summer day in 1939. Bells and flashing lights warn highway traffic, and the small signal on the right tells the motorman that the warning signals are working.

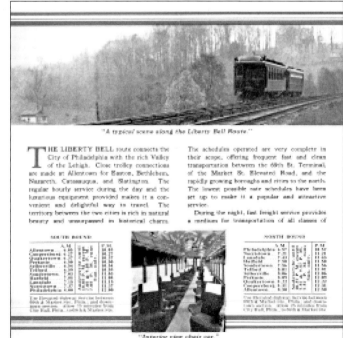

Lehigh Valley Transit Company

Car no. 812 leaves Philadelphia & Western trackage at Norristown, headed for Allentown, on Feb. 6, 1948. D. H. Cope photo/Robert G. Lewis collection.

Snow and the LVT seemed to go together. On Feb. 9, 1936, the A-7 clears the snow at Germantown Pike, just west of Norristown.

A former Dayton & Troy car eastbound in *Easton Limited* service leaves automobile traffic in a trail of blowing snow two days before Christmas, 1945.

Feb. 9, 1936: Snowplow-equipped no. 809, one of 12 cars built by Jewett Car Car Company between 1912 and 1913, enters the north end of Gehmans Siding, halfway between Philadelphia and Allentown. Five of these cars were converted to freight service later in 1939; they served in that capacity until LVT operations ended in 1953.

Lehigh Valley Transit Company

Two William D. Middleton photos from 1950, a mere three years before Lehigh Valley Transit Company would turn its final steel wheel, conclude this chapter. Above, no. 439 was captured at Wales Junction, southbound from Souderton. The date is Feb, 4, 1950. Right: Four months later, on June 4, 1950, a Liberty Bell Limited is descending the southern slope of the Lehigh Mountains just south of Allentown. Car no. 1030 had been acquired from the Indiana Railroad, where its original number was 55.

Lewistown & Reedsville Electric Railway

In this undated photo, two Lewistown & Reedsville cars are at the Square in downtown Lewistown. Photographer unknown/Robert G. Lewis collection.

The Lewistown & Reedsville Electric Railway was built in 1899 on the right-of-way of a 5.9-mile toll road that ran from Lewistown to Reedsville. Four years later it was extended across the Juniata River to connect with the Pennsylvania Railroad at Lewistown Junction. A short branch served the Standard Steel Works at Burnham and an amusement park owned by the L&R. In 1934 the line was abandoned, a victim of highway competition, and parallel service on three weekday round trips by the Kishacoquillas Valley Railway over the PRR's Milroy branch. At is peak, the L&R owned 22 passenger cars.

New Castle
Electric Street Railway

One of New Castle's Birney cars, September 1940.

The New Castle Electric Street Railway operated about 12 miles, mostly in the city streets. Like the Shenango Valley Traction Company (p. 71) in nearby Sharon, it was owned by the Transportation Securities Company of New York. In 1940, the New Castle made attempts to modernize its Birney cars (see accompanying photo at right). A year later, in 1941, bus service was substituted and rail operations were discontinued.

New Castle car no 352 was rebuilt into a "Master Unit Birney" in 1940 by a local master mechanic.

Northumberland County Railway Company

Birney car No. 124 is in Northumberland, headed for the bridge to Sunbury in 1939. James P. Shuman photo/Robert G. Lewis collection.

The Northumberland County Railway Company operated a single-track 3.62-mile line, crossing the broad Susquehanna River on a long bridge from Sunbury to Northumberland. It had seven motor cars and three work cars. The line was abandoned in 1939.

Pennsylvania-New Jersey Railway Company

PNJ car no. 125 is at Trenton, a midpoint on the former line to New Hope, and is ready to return to Yardley.

The Pennsylvania-New Jersey Railway Company, at the time the accompanying photograph was taken at Yardley, Pa., was a remnant of the Bucks County Interurban, which had crossed the Delaware River from Trenton, N.J., to Morrisville, Pa., and continued to Yardville and northwest along the Delaware River to New Hope. A second line went west to Newtown and Doylestown, with a branch from Newtown to Bristol. By 1934, PNJ had been cut down to just 7.25 miles of line from Trenton to Yardley. All service was discontinued Sept. 2, 1934.

PNJ car no. 1 at its terminal in Trenton, N.J., Feb. 13, 1932. While Trenton is its terminal, no. 1 will cross the Delaware River and finish its run in Pennsylvania. William H. Watts, II, photo/Robert G. Lewis collection.

People's Street Railway
of Newport & Nanticoke

Car No. 18, lacking any fender, is thought to have come from the Lowell & Fitchburg Railway in Massachusetts. The photo was taken by William P. Hamilton II, probably in 1929. Robert G. Lewis collection.

The People's Street Railway of Newport & Nanticoke, headquartered at Wanamie, operated 8.5 miles of line with its roster of 12 passenger cars and five work cars. All service ended following a head-on collision in April 1935. Not much is known about this obscure line.

The mining town of Nanticoke is best known as the home of Pete Gray (Wyshner), baseball's "One Arm Wonder." He was right-handed until he lost his right arm at age 6 in 1921, when he slipped while riding on a farmer's wagon and his right arm was caught in the spokes. The arm had to be amputated above the elbow. Gray's love of baseball led him to learn to bat and field one-handed, catching the ball in his glove and then quickly removing his glove and transferring the ball to his hand in one motion. Gray played for such semi-pro teams as the Memphis Chicks of the Southern Association and the Brooklyn Bushwicks. The St. Louis Browns purchased Gray's contract in 1945 from the Memphis Chicks. Wearing no. 14, he played left and center field, appearing in 77 games, batting .218. On May 19, the one-armed rookie collected five hits and two RBIs as the Browns swept the Yankees.

Gray's life story was chronicled in the 1986 television movie "A Winner Never Quits."

Philadelphia & West Chester Traction Company

P&WC car no. 84, built by Brill in 1932—a very modern car for its time—moves onto the double-track midway on the line to Media, March 7, 1953.

The Philadelphia & West Chester Traction Company operated two lines out of 69th Street Terminal, and each line had a short branch. The longer of the two lines was the 19-mile line to West Chester, with a five-mile branch from Llanarch, two miles out of 69th Street to Ardmore. Much of the West Chester line was laid alongside the West Chester Pike, ending on the street in downtown West Chester. The second line ran from 69th street to Media, 8.5 miles, with a 2.3-mile branch from Drexel Hill, two miles out of 69th Street, to Sharon Hill.

The West Chester line was abandoned beyond Llanarch on June 6, 1954, and the track was torn up in order to widen the Pike. No bus substitution was made. The Ardmore line ended rail service Dec. 30, 1966, and was later paved. Buses operated over the private right-of-way beginning March 31, 1967.

In 1936, the P&WCT changed its name to Philadelphia Suburban Transportation Company and promoted its operations as the "Red Arrow Lines." In 1968, the company was sold to SEPTA. Before abandonment of the West Chester line, system mileage totaled 51, and car ownership was 53, plus 11 service cars.

Philadelphia & West Chester Traction Company

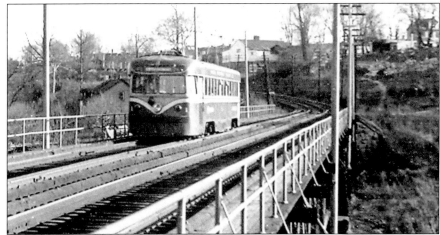

P&WC car no. 1 is on the bridge over Darby Creek at Clifton on the Sharon Hill line, March 7, 1953.

Above: P&WC car no. 43 carries white flags. It is on charter to the National Railway Historical Society, March 6, 1941, and has just departed from Drexel Hill station on the line to Media. The Sharon Hill line branches off to its right.

PHILADELPHIA
AND
WEST CHESTER
TRACTION CO.

TIME TABLE

Daily and Sunday

CARS BETWEEN

PHILADELPHIA (69th St. Terminal)

AND

Newtown Square—West Chester
Highland Park—Llanerch—Brookline—Ardmore
Clifton—Aldan—Collingdale—Sharon Hill
Drexel Hill—Springfield—Media

During rush hours and on Saturdays, Sundays and Holidays, additional cars will be run when necessary.

Cars stop only on signal at points designated by signs reading "CAR STOP" and stations. Signal should be given by passenger distinctly and in ample time for motorman to stop car at landing.

The connections shown are given for the benefit of patrons, but this Company will not be responsible for connections, errors or changes.

SCHEDULE IN EFFECT MARCH 27, 1932

SUBJECT TO CHANGE WITHOUT NOTICE

1932 Philadelphia & West Chester timetable.

Philadelphia & West Chester Traction Company

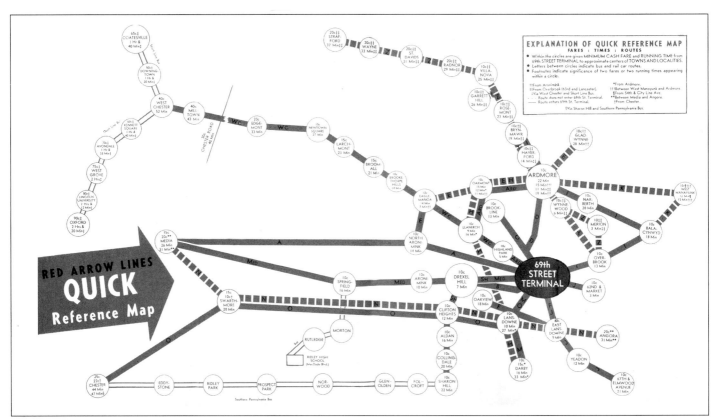

RED ARROW
TRANSIT GUIDE

to Philadelphia's
Beautiful Western Suburbs

SPEED—COMFORT
SAFETY—COURTESY

PHILADELPHIA SUBURBAN
TRANSPORTATION COMPANY
ARONIMINK TRANSPORTATION COMPANY

General Offices—69th St. Terminal
Upper Darby, Pa.
Copyright 1939

Brill's last interurban cars were these shovel-nosed streamliners delivered in 1941. Dubbed "Bond Bread" cars for their resemblance to the popular sandwich loaf of the day, Brill designed them to compete with the PCC car. They were derived from Brill's lightweight, high-speed, one-man 80 Series cars of 1932. P&WC car no. 6, by this time operating as Philadelphia Suburban Transportation Company, is still in its original maroon, black, and silver livery. It's seen here on an icy Dec. 21, 1945—the first postwar Christmas season—westbound at Springfield Road on its way to Media. Notice the cookie-cutter suburban homes. They would grow in numbers as veterans returned home from World War II and bought houses, assisted by the GI housing bill. No. 6 would survive until SEPTA retired her in 1981 to make way for "modern" light rail vehicles.

P&WC car no. 61 heads a two-car train at Drexel Hill on a snowy Dec. 21, 1945.

P&WC car no. 4 is towing disabled No. 11 eastward along the West Chester Pike after a late winter snowstorm, March 8, 1953.

Philadelphia & Western Railway

The hallmark of the P&W was its ten Brill-built "Bullet" cars. No. 200 is eastbound, approaching Ardmore Junction, on Feb. 12, 1936. What could possibly be sleeker and more beautiful than a Brill Bullet, which looked like it was moving, even when stopped? The Brill Bullets—in 1929, the first railcars designed in a wind tunnel, in order to reduce electric power consumption while reducing headways—remained in service until 1992. Tested at 100-plus mph, they operated at 80-85 mph in regular service, cutting Norristown Express schedules from 24 minutes to only 16 minutes while consuming about 40% less electric power than the equipment they replaced.

The Philadelphia & Western Railway's first line was built from the 69th & Market Street Terminal in Upper Darby to Strafford, 11.1 miles, in 1907 as part of the grand scheme of financier Jay Gould to built a Philadelphia-Chicago line to compete with the Pennsylvania Railroad. The P&W's line from Villanova to Norristown was built in 1912, and became the main line, connecting with Lehigh Valley Transit (p. 33) at Norristown. The Strafford line was abandoned in March 1956.

The P&W, best known for its landmark, high speed, streamlined "Brill Bullet" cars, was sold to Philadelphia Suburban Transportation Company, now part of SEPTA, on Dec. 31, 1953. Today, it's SEPTA Route 100, the Norristown High Speed Line.

The definitive book on the P&W is CERA Bulletin 140, "Pig & Whistle: The Story of the Philadelphia & Western Railway," by Ronald DeGraw.

November 1931: P&W car no. 29 is leading a two-car train ready to depart from Norristown station before the present elevated station was built. A Lehigh Valley Transit car is in the rear. William H. Watts, II, photo/Robert G. Lewis collection.

Here's something a little more contemporary: A two-car train of former Chicago elevated cars is departing SEPTA's Bryn Mawr station, eastbound, on June 24, 1988. Fred W. Schneider photo/Robert G. Lewis collection.

Philadelphia Rapid Transit

Left: "Nearside" car no. 6719 is southbound on 22nd Street approaching Allegheny Avenue in 1936. It is crossing the Reading Railroad's double-track line to Norristown. That line, then recently electrified with 11,000-volt a.c., created a complicated overhead crossing with PRT's 600-volt d.c. traction system.

The Philadelphia Rapid Transit Company—the "PRT" as Philadelphians called it—was by all measures the largest street railway operator in Pennsylvania.

In 1934, the PRT operated 2,914 motorized cars and 250 service cars over a 581-mile system. It also operated the city's subway and elevated lines. An interesting system of suburban trolley lines served Delaware County connecting with city lines at Darby. They were operated exclusively by Birney cars. All of the lines were single-track, and operated mostly alongside county roads or on private rights-of-way.

Trolley operations today are SEPTA's light rail lines operating over the so-called "subway/surface lines" that reach central Philadelphia on tracks paralleling the 69th Street-Frankford subway-elevated line, and a recently revived Girard Avenue line running 15 miles cross-town from Frankford to West Philadelphia.

Company

February 1934: Four-wheel Birney car no. 1013, built in 1919 by American Car Company, crosses Providence Road onto Rose Valley Road in Nether Providence Township, on the Route 71 Media-Folsom line. All but two of these cars were scrapped when this line was abandoned on Aug. 14, 1938.

A Route 77 Birney car heads south from Media to Chester along Park Avenue in Middletown Township. The photo was taken from a Pennsylvania Railroad bridge on the PRR's Media line in April 1936.

Philadelphia Rapid Transit Company

Above: A Route 17 car southbound alongside Essington Ave., headed for Chester, crosses Darby Creek on a primitive drawbridge in 1934. Boaters had to call a day ahead to request a bridge opening.

Left: A Birney car on PRT's Route 72 in September 1938 would be recalled 20 years later when Bob Lewis journeyed across the Trans-Siberian Railroad.

Two PRT routes—Route 55 and Route 6—served Willow Grove Park, Philadelphia's premier amusement facility. Both originated at the Broad Street Subway's Broad-Olney terminal. Brill-built car nos. 8055, 8040, and 8035 wait at multi-tracked Willow Grove terminal on a hot July 10, 1938. Route 55 to Willow Grove lasted until September 1940. Route 6 survived until 1958. The park became a shopping mall.

April 10, 1938: In sharp contrast to Route 72's bleak countryside, PRT car no. 8055, on Route 55, rolls through Jenkintown along Old York Road beside great estates on its way from Willow Grove to the Broad-Olney terminal, where it connected with the Broad Street Subway.

Pittsburgh, Harmony, Butler &

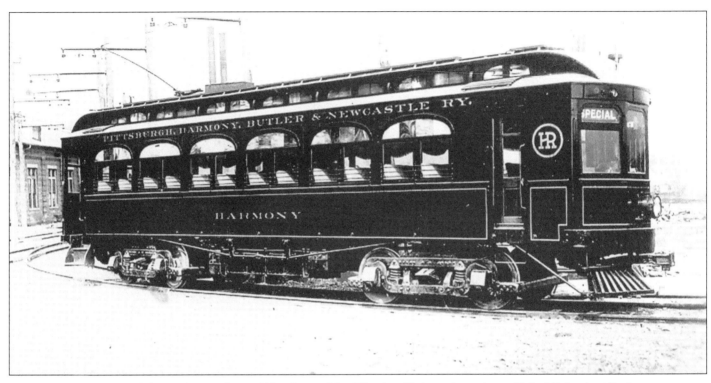

The "Harmony" was a special excursion car that could be chartered for $55 a day. Photographer unknown/Robert G. Lewis collection.

The Pittsburgh, Harmony, Butler & New Castle Railway Company, which opened in 1908, was best known as the "Harmony Line." Not all names on the map were actual stops. When the company was acquiring the right-of-way, cutting through privately held land, each landowner was promised a flag stop. An express service trolley, which operated at 65 or more mph, stopped at the main stations. Cars ran into Pittsburgh, with Pittsburgh Railway employees (p. 58) completing the trip from the interchange. Freight service consisted mostly of farmers shipping fresh milk, cheese, eggs, poultry, and fruits and vegetables to Pittsburgh markets.

By 1927, the PHB&NC operated 85 miles of 5-foot 2-1/2-inch gauge track with overhead voltages of 1,200 volts d.c. and 600 volts d.c. That year, its roster consisted of 25 passenger cars, six motor freights, two work cars, and 58 trailer freight cars. All 25 passenger cars were shipped disassembled to the Harmony car barn from the St. Louis Car Company for assembly with locally manufactured wheels.

Operations ended between Pittsburgh and Butler on the railway's Butler Short Line section on April 22, 1931. The Harmony Route lasted a few more months. The final car arrived at the Harmony car barn at 4:48 a.m. Aug. 15, 1931—a short life for such an elegant interurban system.

A Harmony Line interurban car could carry about 40 passengers. Car no. 114 is on a trestle near Elwood City. Sister car no. 115, the only PHB&NC car that survives today, is at the Arden Trolley Museum in Washington, Pa. Photographer unknown/Robert G. Lewis collection.

New Castle Railway Company

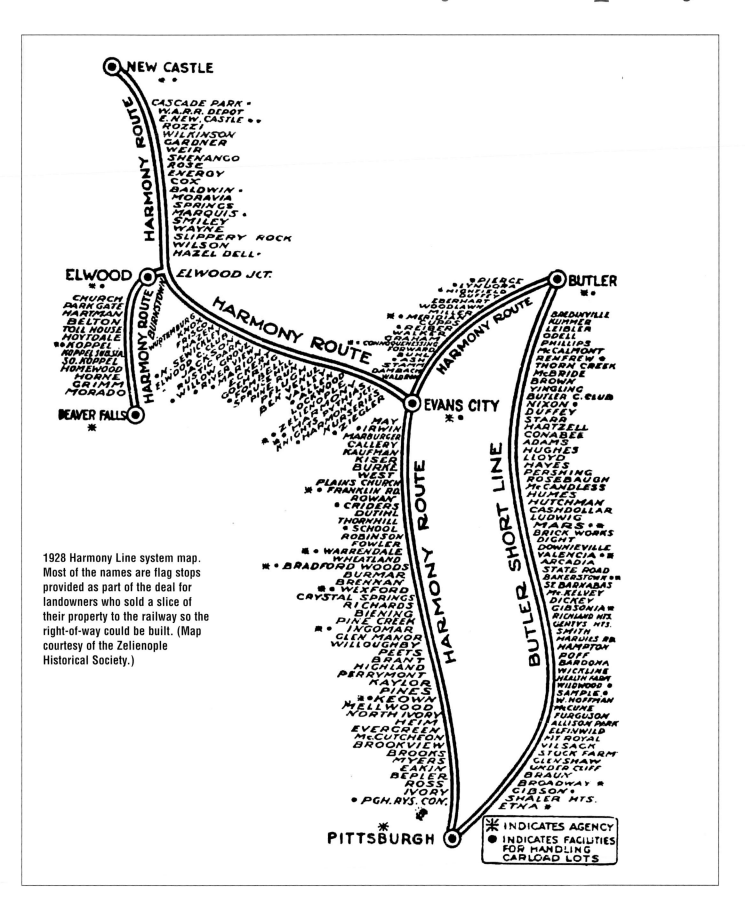

1928 Harmony Line system map. Most of the names are flag stops provided as part of the deal for landowners who sold a slice of their property to the railway so the right-of-way could be built. (Map courtesy of the Zelienople Historical Society.)

Pittsburgh Railways Company

May 12, 1940: One of Pittsburgh Railway's interurban cars is midway on the Washington line, taking the siding for a car from Pittsburgh.

Pittsburgh Railways Company — WEEKLY STREET CAR PASS

GOOD ONLY FROM **Oct. 12th to Oct. 18th, 1930, Incl.**

GOOD FROM 5.00 A.M. SUNDAY UNTIL 5.00 A.M. THE FOLLOWING SUNDAY

Passengers showing this within the FIRST FARE TERURBAN CARS during shown above. These zones be reached by a token fare Pittsburgh. Pass is to be Operator when fare should One Passenger per trip and of rider during entire trip.

42

pass will be permitted to ride ZONE on any car except IN the seven (7) day period include all points which can from downtown district of shown to Conductor or Car bo p... t is good for but it is to ...In in possession

NOT GOOD ON SPECIAL OR PICNIC CARS

W

PRICE $1.50 PUNCH CUT

NOT REDEEMABLE **69319**

Commercial Manager

Pittsburgh Railways Company, formed in 1902 from the merger of several railways, was the second-largest traction company in the Commonwealth of Pennsylvania. In 1934, it operated 582 miles of standard-gauge lines on 68 routes in Pittsburgh and its environs. It owned 1,032 motorized cars and 18 trailers, 8 freight cars and 148 service cars—numbers surpassed only by Philadelphia Rapid Transit. In addition to its extensive network of city and suburban lines, there were two interurban routes, one to Washington, about 32 miles, and one to Charleroi and Roscoe, about 48 miles.

Pittsburgh Railways successor Port Authority of Allegheny County (PAT) operates a greatly reduced rail system. Only three of the original lines—the 42, 47 and 52—survive as rail routes, but those lines have been completely rebuilt and equipped with modern light rail vehicles. Lines within the city have gone underground, and an extension under the Allegheny River to the west side is under construction. Most of the other lines are now PAT bus routes, but they have retained their original route numbers.

The accompanying photographs were taken in the 1930s, a time when Pittsburgh Railways cars reached nearly every neighborhood in the city and its suburbs, and its two interurban lines provided fast, frequent service.

"Something brand new on wheels"

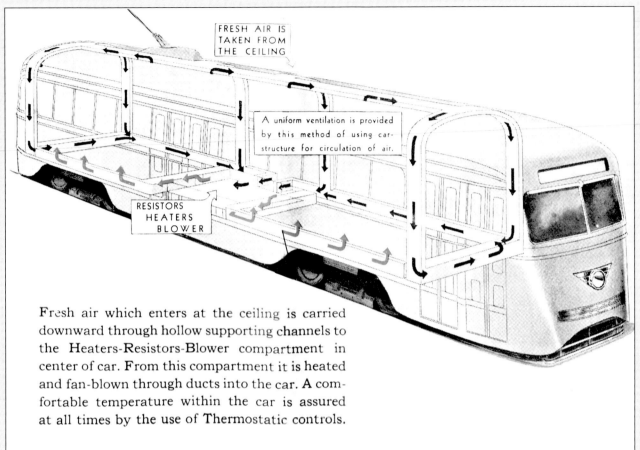

FRESH AIR IS TAKEN FROM THE CEILING

A uniform ventilation is provided by this method of using car-structure for circulation of air.

RESISTORS HEATERS BLOWER

Fresh air which enters at the ceiling is carried downward through hollow supporting channels to the Heaters-Resistors-Blower compartment in center of car. From this compartment it is heated and fan-blown through ducts into the car. A comfortable temperature within the car is assured at all times by the use of Thermostatic controls.

In 1937, Pittsburgh Railways took delivery of its first two orders of PCC cars, 201 cars in all. Eventually, the system boasted 666 PCCs, which it called (in keeping with the times) "Streamline Cars," on its roster—the second largest PCC fleet in North America. A 1937 brochure introduced the new cars to the public in glowing terms:

Smoothness rides the rails in 1937 with the new streamline trolleys. The first 100 cars are now in operation. The first of the second 100 are now in town.

When the first of the Streamline Cars began regular operation, in 1937, Pittsburghers experienced the thrill of a sensationally new riding comfort. Nothing like it had ever before come to town. . . . It was an innovation in street car travel. Never had any street car glided along so smoothly and quietly. . . . Never had street car seats felt so deep and comfortable. . . . Never had street car lighting been so bright and cheerful and easy-to-read by. . . . Never had any street car offered so many surprising advantages. Here was something brand new on wheels, and as shipments of that first 100 arrived in town and were placed in operation, they were enthusiastically acclaimed.

Now, another 100 have started to arrive. Streamline Cars, fresh from the factory, have already been placed in operation on the No. 69 Squirrel Hill Route, and make up the entire base schedule, with other type cars being added only during the rush hours. Shipments are being hurried and just as soon as cars of this second 100 are received, they will be put in operation.

With this extra order of cars, the same "new riding comfort" that was the feature of the original 100 . . . the same Streamline design with additional refinements, becomes available to more people on more routes throughout the system. Soon, a grand total of 201 Streamline Cars will be providing Pittsburghers with transportation and equipment among the most modern of its kind in the world.

Giddap and GO

Pittsburgh Railways Company

September 1941: PCC car no. 1178 is on the loop at Millvale, ready for the return run to Pittsburgh's downtown, the Golden Triangle. Hopefully, the missing motorman is not patronizing the Rathskeller in the background!

PCC car no. 1297 is westbound at Crafton on the Carnegie line in 1941.

Pottstown Passenger Railway

Aug. 2, 1936: Pottstown Passenger Railway "semi-convertible" (in this case, "see-through") car no. 111 spans Sanatoga Road and a crossing east of Pottstown.

Pottstown Passenger Railway (did any other trolley system call itself a "passenger railway"?), at the time of its abandonment on Oct. 1, 1936, operated a 5.5-mile standard-gauge line from Stowe, on the north end of town, to Linfield on the south end. Most of its track ran through Pottstown, down the center of State Route 422. PPR had only six cars. They were "semi-convertible" cars built by Brill in 1915: Their sides were rolled up into the roof in fair weather to make them "open cars." They were also known as "see through" cars.

Still chasing car no. 111 as it heads east alongside State Highway 422, having gotten a white light from the Nachod signal on the pole to its left. That's the 1936 Chevrolet Standard Coupe of William H. Watts, II, Bob Lewis's frequent traveling companion on traction expeditions, in the background.

Pottstown Passenger Railway

Two more scenes of car no. 111 from Aug. 2, 1936, two months before the Pottstown Passenger Railway ceased operations. Above, 111 is being readied for a run while two sister cars enjoy the shelter of the PPR's wooden car barn at the eastern end of Pottstown. At this location, the transition from side-of-road right-of-way to running in the center of the street occurred. Inset: No. 111 is headed eastbound toward Stowe at the Eden Street turnout. Sister car no. 110 is in the background. The front end of these cars was typical for Brill's post-World War I trolleys. Note the retriever mechanism used for raising and lowering the trolley pole, adjacent to the headlight.

Reading Street Railway

Reading Street Railway car no. 370 is at the end of the Stoney Creek line on March 4, 1935, during a National Railway Historical Society special excursion.

In 1934, the Reading Street Railway Company operated 80 miles of streetcar lines reaching out in all directions from Reading to Mohnton, on a line that once went on to Adamston and connected there with Conestoga Traction (p. 12) for Lancaster:

• To Womelsdorf.

• To Kutztown, connecting there with the Allentown & Reading (p. 9).

• To Birdsboro and, over the wholly owned Oley Valley Railway, to Boyertown, connecting there for Pottstown, Norristown, and Philadelphia.

A separate division operated from Lebanon to Annville, connecting there with Hershey Transit (p. 20). The company operated a fleet of 120 cars, plus 25 work cars, in 1934. On Jan. 9, 1952, all rail operations were terminated.

Car no. 86 at Temple, March 24, 1935. The Reading Railroad's Temple station is in the background, on the right.

Traction and steam! In 1941, car no. 307 is at Temple, the shortened terminus of the abandoned line to Kutztown. A Reading Railroad merchandise freight rolls along the railroad's Reading-Allentown main line. J.H. Richards photo/Robert G. Lewis collection.

Here's an original, punched Reading Street Railway ticket from one of Bob Lewis's excursions in 1935. The Globe Ticket Company of Philadelphia printed this ticket. The company, founded in 1868, is known today as the Globe Ticket and Label Company, and has numerous locations in the U.S.

A description from the company's website, www.globeticket.com, reads: "Globe Ticket has chronicled major events in the history of the United States. From the Ringling Brothers Circus circa 1870, to the Woodstock Music Festival, to Muhammad Ali's return fight in Atlanta, to the commemorative Braves tickets for Hank Aaron's 715th home run, Globe has been a part."

READING ST. RWY. COMPANY	TIME	
	1	15
THIS TRANSFER Acceptable only as Designated on the Reverse Side within Time Limit or first connection thereafter on Date of Issuance.	30	45
	2	15
	30	45
	3	15
	30	45
	4	15
Transfer Issued From	30	45
- COACH -	5	15
NORTH	30	45
EAST	6	
SOUTH	30	45
WEST	7	15
	30	45
10c FARE	8	15
- RAILWAY -	30	45
SCHYL. A	9	15
4th ST. LOOP	30	45
5th & 6th ST.	10	15
TEMPLE	30	45
MOHNTON	11	15
PERKIOMEN	30	45
EMERGENCY	12	15
A. M. IF COUPON IS DETACHED	30	45

26479

P.M.

VOID IF DETACHED

GLOBE TICKET COMPANY, PHILA., PA.

— COACH LINES —

FROM	TO	AT
Reiffton Jacksonwald	Jacksonwald Reiffton	Junction
Reiffton or Jacksonwald	N. 23rd St. W. Perk. Ave.	23rd & Perk.
Pennside	E. Perk. Ave.	23rd & Perk.
West Lawn Reading Blv'd.	Reading Blv'd. West Lawn	First Avenue
6th & Amity Temple	Temple 6th & Amity	5th & Spring
Temple Centre Ave.	4th St. Loop Temple	Centre & Greenwich
Temple	Riverside	5th & Windsor
Grill Cotton St.	Cotton St. Grill	5 & Bingaman

NOTE: Birdsboro passengers desiring to transfer to Pennside, or vice versa, will alight at 23rd & Fairview Streets, and walk to 23rd & Perkiomen Avenue. Hampden B'lv'd. Line passengers will transfer at intersecting Coach and Car Lines.

— CAR LINES —

FROM	TO	AT
Shillington	North 4th St. Temp.-Sch.Ave	4 & Washington
4th St. Loop 6th & Amity	6th & Amity 4th St. Loop	Centre & Greenwich
Schy'l Avenue	N'theast Loop 10th Street	10th & Elm
Riverside	Temple	6th & Bern
Cotton Street 6th & Amity	6th & Amity Riverside	4 & Windsor
Mohnton Cotton Street	Cotton Street Mohnton	5 & Bingaman
Mohnton	Riverside	6 & Washington
Cotton Street E. Perk. Ave.	E. Perk. Ave. Cotton Street	19 & Perkiomen
Cotton Street Temple	Temple Riverside	6 & Windsor
N. 5th Street	S. 5th Street	5 & Washington

NOTE: Fourth St. Loop or Riverside passengers desiring to transfer to Temple Line will transfer to Sixth & Amity car at 4th & Greenwich Sts. and then transfer at 6th & Amity Sts. to the Temple Line.
ALL OTHER TRANSFER POINTS WILL BE WHERE LINES INTERSECT ON PENN STREET.

Roxborough, Chestnut Hill
& Norristown Railway

RCH&N car nos. 103 and 105 meet at Plymouth Meeting, Dec. 12, 1931—the day before service ended for good. Brill built both these cars in 1916. William H. Watts, II, photo/Robert G. Lewis collection.

The Roxborough, Chestnut Hill & Norristown Railway had two connections with the Philadelphia Rapid Transit (p. 52), one at Wissahickon, the other at Chestnut Hill. These two lines joined at Barren Hill for the journey to Norristown, with a branch from Plymouth Meeting to Conshocken, and a short line across the Schuylkill River to Swedeland. By 1931, the track was in poor condition, as the 8.0-mile ride from Chestnut Hill to Main & DeKalb Street in Norristown took 38 minutes.

All RCH&N and connecting Schuylkill Valley Traction Company were part of the Reading Transit Company, but were operated separately.

Service on all lines ended Dec. 13, 1931.

Schuylkill Valley Traction car No. 191 at Bridgeport, across the river from Norristown, Aug. 25, 1931. William H. Watts, II, photo/Robert G. Lewis collection.

Scranton & Binghamton Railroad Company

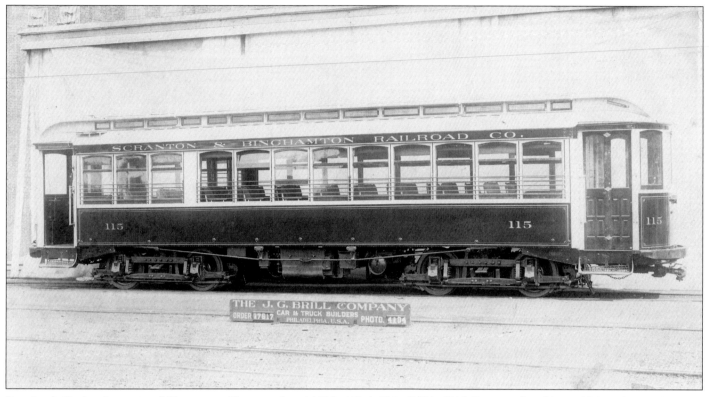

Scranton & Binghamton car no. 115 was one of four, numbered 115 to 118, built by Brill in 1911. It was equipped for multiple-unit operation. This Brill builder's photo shows it was car order no. 17617. Note the three-window smoking compartment. Robert G. Lewis collection.

The Scranton & Binghamton Railroad Company never reached Binghamton, N.Y.. At Foster, about halfway, it turned northwest, and went upward to Montrose, 46 miles from Scranton. Only three trips per day went the entire distance to Montrose in the 1920s. These trips were described as "milk and express cars," though frequent trips were made as far as Factoryville. Entrance to Scranton was by trackage rights over Scranton Transit (p. 68) for 2.33 miles. Service ended in 1932, when the cars were scrapped and the tracks removed.

Herbert T. Lewis, Bob Lewis's father, recalled a trip from Montrose to Scranton in 1930. He was the only passenger on the final trip of the day, and rode the head end at the motorman's invitation.

Scranton Transit Company

Scranton Transit car no. 501, one of 10 "Electromobile" cars built by Osgood Bradley in 1929, is operating in 1934 on the Green Ridge suburban line, the last line in service before abandonment in 1954

Scranton Transit Company arguably was America's first electric-powered transit operator, providing revenue service in 1886 before the pioneer system in Richmond, Va., was collecting fares. In 1934, when Bob Lewis took the photo above, the railway was operating 100 cars over about 62 route-miles. On Dec. 18, 1954, all rail services were discontinued.

Scranton's current provider of public transportation is the County of Lackawanna Transit System (COLTS), whose buses provide service within the city and limited service that reaches in all directions to Carbondale, Daleville, Pittston, and Fleetville.

Cincinnati-built car no. 355 at Old Forge, March 7, 1943. The 355, built in 1911, soldiered on until it was scrapped in 1947. William H. Watts, II, photo/Robert G. Lewis collection.

Shamokin & Mount Carmel Transit Company

Shamokin & Mount Carmel Transit Company car no. 16 at the company's carbarn in Kulmont, July 5, 1936. No. 16 was built by Brill for the Eastern Massachusetts Street Railway, and came to the S&MtC in 1921.

The Shamokin & Mount Carmel Transit Company was among the pioneer traction companies, not just in Pennsylvania, but in the nation. In November 1894, service commenced between the two cities in its name, a distance of 10 miles. Later, the railway was extended east to Centralia and Ashland, and a short branch was built from Mount Carmel to Locust Gap.

Service between Shamokin & Mount Carmel ended on July 2, 1936, but continued on the short branch to Locust Gap until March 20, 1937. At the time of abandonment, 20 passenger cars were on the railway's active roster.

Double-truck lightweight car westbound along 15th Street, on its run from Mt. Carmel to Shamokin. Early 1930s photo by Jim Richards/Robert G. Lewis collection.

Shamokin & Mount Carmel Transit Company

July 5, 1936: Birney car no. 120 is at Mount Carmel at the end of its run through the heart of Pennsylvania coal country. Both trolley poles are up, as the ends are being changed for the trip back to Locust Gap. The connecting bus to Shamokin is loading at the curb.

Birney car no. 120 is at the end of the line in Locust Gap, July 5, 1936, three days after all other operations had ceased. This line would be abandoned on March 20, 1937.

Car no. 4 just west of Mt. Carmel enroute to Shamokin; the Pennsylvania Railroad is in the foreground. Early 1930s photo by Jim Richards/Robert G. Lewis collection.

Shenango Valley
Traction Company

Shenango Valley Birney car no. 170 on the loop at the end of the State Street line in September 1940.

In 1934, the Shenango Valley Traction Company operated 14 miles of line in Sharon. Like the nearby New Castle Electric Street Railway (p. 41), it was owned by the Transportation Securities Company of New York. Thirty cars were on its roster. All trolley service was discontinued in 1941.

Skippack & Perkiomen Transit Company

Skippack & Perkiomen Transit Company car no. 4, one of four cars built by Brill.
Builder's photo/Robert G. Lewis collection.

The Skippack & Perkiomen Transit Company, originally Montgomery Transit, operated a 13-mile line from Trooper to Harleysville, using the tracks of the Schuylkill Valley Company to reach Norristown from Trooper, a distance of three miles.

Brill built three unusual cars for the S&PTC. They were only 33 feet, 6 inches long, but had a smoking compartment with longitudinal seats at one end. This little line also operated a freight service in cooperation with Reading Street Railway (p. 64) and Philadelphia Rapid Transit (p. 52), handling farm and dairy products south and general freight north. Most of the railway's trackage ran alongside Montgomery Pike. Despite its enterprising ways, this small operation was an early victim of highway competition. It abandoned operations in June 1925.

Car no. 4 seated 36, eight in a smoking section separated from the main compartment by a swinging door. Builder's photo/Robert G. Lewis collection.

Southern Pennsylvania Traction Company

Trim Southern Pennsylvania car no. 509 at Cragmere Road, just north of Wilmington, Del., on Sept. 4, 1934. The 509, a multiple-unit car similar to Philadelphia Rapid Transit's but with heavier trucks, was built by Brill in 1918.

The Southern Pennsylvania Traction Company operated only two lines. Its main line extended 16 miles from Wilmington, Del., to Darby, Pa., where it connected with the lines of the Philadelphia Rapid Transit (p. 52). A six-mile branch line ran from Chester to Media. The main line was abandoned on Dec. 15, 1934.

Steubenville, East Liverpool & Beaver Valley

SEL&BV car "Steubenville" at Irondale Road between Stratton and Wellsville, Ohio, Feb. 22, 1936.

The Steubenville, East Liverpool & Beaver Valley Traction Company operated a line between Steubenville, Ohio, and Beaver, Pa., a distance of 43 miles, the northeastern third of which was in the Keystone State. Connecting steam train service to Pittsburgh over the Pittsburgh & Lake Erie Railroad at Beaver was advertised in its timetables; the interurbans must have run very close to schedule, for some of the trips allowed but one or two minutes for the connection. Local service was operated out of Steubenville. The railway was called "The Stream Line."

Six modern cars from the G. C. Kuhlman Car Co., given names instead of numbers, covered through services. These cars went to the Lehigh Valley Transit (p. 33), where they were assigned numbers 430 through 435, after SEL&BV service ended. The line was abandoned June 30, 1938.

This April 28, 1929 map and timetable show the SEL&BV's quick connection to Pittsburgh & Lake Erie steam trains at Beaver.

Corrected to April 28th, 1929

(Subject to Change Without Notice)

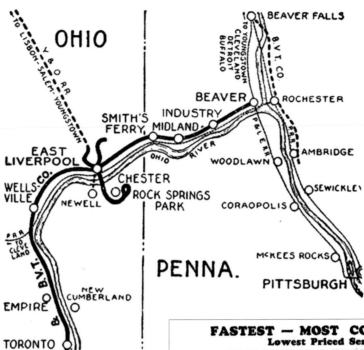

FASTEST — MOST CONVENIENT
Lowest Priced Service
EAST LIVERPOOL TO PITTSBURGH
(Eastern Standard Time)

Car Leaves E. Liverpool	Arrives Beaver	Train Leaves Beaver	Arrives Pittsburgh
A.M. 5 30	A.M. 6 25	A.M. *6 28	A.M. *7 00
		*6 33	*7 15
6 00	6 55	6 59	7 55
7 00	7 55	7 57	8 40
8 00	8 55	9 15	10 10
10 00	10 55	11 07	11 40
10 30	11 25	11 44	P.M. 12 45
P.M. 1 00	P.M. 1 55	P.M. 2 03	2 50
2 00	2 55	3 04	4 05
2 30	3 25	3 43	4 20
3 00	3 55	3 57	4 40
3 30	4 25	4 32	5 26
4 00	4 55	4 58	5 35
4 30	5 25	*5 34	*6 25
5 30	6 25	6 46	7 25
6 00	6 55	7 12	7 50
8 00	8 55	8 59	9 40
9 00	9 55	10 06	10 55

Pittsburgh to East Liverpool

Train Leaves Pittsburgh	Arrives Beaver	Car Leaves Beaver	Arrives E. Liverpool
A.M. 4 50	A.M. 5 54	A.M. 6 12	A.M. 7 05
*6 10	*7 05	7 12	8 05
8 10	8 41	8 42	9 35
8 15	9 08	9 12	10 05
10 00	10 32	10 42	11 35
11 00	11 45	P.M. 12 12	P.M. 1 05
11 55	P.M. 12 52	1 12	2 05
P.M. 12 45	1 18	1 42	2 35
2 10	2 47	3 12	4 05
*2 15	*3 15	3 42	4 35
4 00	4 34	4 42	5 35
*4 20	*5 02	5 12	6 05
*4 45	*5 40	5 43	6 35
6 00	6 33	6 42	7 35
8 00	8 33	8 42	9 35
8 45	9 42	9 42	10 35
10 00	10 34	10 42	11 35
10 50	11 43	11 45	A.M. 12 05

*—Daily except Sunday. Best connections in dark type.

Fare — East Liverpool to Pittsburgh — 91c
Tickets for 12 trips between East Liverpool and Beaver cost $4.50. Tickets for 10 trips between Beaver and Pittsburgh cost $5.27. These tickets are good for three months and may be used by any number of persons.

The Steubenville, East Liverpool & Beaver Valley Traction Co.

EAST LIVERPOOL, OHIO

Sunbury & Selinsgrove Electric

S&S car nos.102 and 103 were brought over from the Sunbury & Northumberland during bankruptcy proceedings around 1908. Date and photographer unknown/Gene Gordon collection.

The Sunbury & Selinsgrove Electric Street Railway Company operated a 6.2-mile line connecting the towns in its name, which were located on opposite sides of the Susquehanna River. The trolleys shared a two-lane toll bridge that spanned the river. Operations began in May 1908, after reorganization of the bankrupt Sunbury & Northumberland Railway, and ended with the closing of the line on Dec. 31, 1934.

S&S car no. 114 at the Hummels Wharf carbarn two weeks before abandonment on Dec. 15, 1934. Howard Johnston photo/Gene Gordon collection.

Below: Car no. 116 is at Market Square in downtown Sunbury in this undated photo by Frank Goldsmith/Gene Gordon collection.

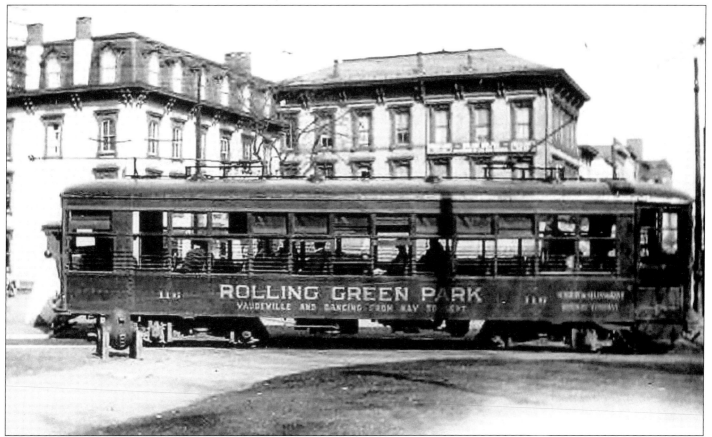

Tarentum, Brackenridge & Butler Street Railway

Car no. 103 near the end of the line in Birdville, April 1940.

As first an editor and later Publisher of Railway Age and other industry trade magazines, Bob Lewis's unwritten yet frequently invoked rule was "avoid using superlatives. They can get you in trouble." However, in the case of the Tarentum, Brackenridge & Butler Street Railway, it was in some ways unique. Right up to the last day of service in 1940, its single-truck cars ran without air brakes. A track brake, like those used on the West Penn lines, protected them as they descended a steep grade onto a sharp curve into downtown Tarentum. While the line was projected to run northwest to Butler, about 24 miles, only the first 3.38 miles to Birdville were ever built.

TB&B car no. 103 descends a steep grade—without air brakes—into downtown Tarentum.

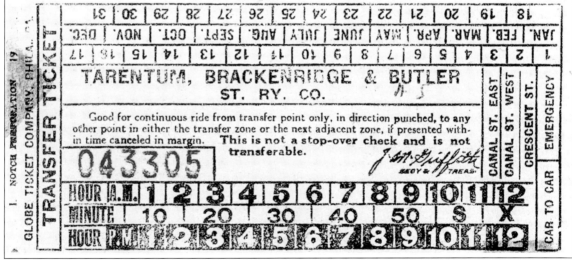

Here's another example of a fare instrument printed by the Globe Ticket Company of Elk Grove Village, Ill. (see p. 65 for more information). This particular example is from 1919 and appears to be unpunched. Robert G. Lewis collection.

Valley Railways Company

After Valley Railways had discontinued all trolley service in April 1938, car nos. 80, 24, and 27 were out of service awaiting the scrapper's torch. No. 80 had been built in 1917, the 24 and the 27 in 1913, all by Brill.

The Valley Railways Company had its headquarters, carbarn, and shops in Lemoyne, across the Susquehanna River from Harrisburg. At the time of its abandonment in April 1938, 15.8 miles of 5 foot, 2 inch gauge route-miles were in service. Equipment had been reduced to six passenger cars and four service cars.

Below: Valley Railways car no. 82 is at West End Junction on July 25, 1932. The 82 was built by Brill in 1917, wrecked in December 1932, and scrapped in 1933. William H. Watts, II, photo/Robert G. Lewis collection.

West Penn Railways

Familiar with the expression, "A pig doesn't have to change trains in Chicago—but *you* do!"? Well, here we have West Penn 212 and Pittsburgh Railways 4318 exchanging passengers at Trafford. Passengers had to change cars. Freight cars ran through!

The West Penn's traction lines thoroughly covered the coal and coke region in Westmoreland and Fayette counties just east and southeast of Pittsburgh. A connection with Pittsburgh Railways (p. 58) at Trafford provided an easy transfer of passengers and through running of a trolley freight service.

Most of the West Penn's network of 339 miles was Pennsylvania Broad Gauge (5 feet, 2-1/2 inches) on private rights-of-way or along the side of county roads. There was one standard-gauge line. The West Penn controlled the Allegheny Valley Street Railway Company, which, in 1934, operated a single line along the west bank of the Allegheny River between Aspinwall, where it connected with Pittsburgh Railways (p. 58) to Tarentum and Natrona, about

16 miles. It also operated five non-contiguous lines, among them one in the Wheeling, W.Va., region. (See the map on p. 84.) The company was headquartered in Greensburg, Pa.

The West Penn's car fleet, mostly large, steel center-door cars painted traction orange, serviced a network of lines that missed few communities in the two counties. A distinctive feature of its cars was that they had no air brakes; cars were brought to a low speed by regenerative track brakes and to a stop by hand brakes worked by the motorman. In 1934, the West Penn owned 105 passenger cars, 14 freight cars, and 32 service cars.

There were no other trolley lines quite like the West Penn; it was a joy to ride. Alas, the last cars went to the big car barn in Connellsville on Aug. 9, 1952.

Keystone State Traction's cover photo: West Penn's big center-door car no.727 hurries eastward from Brownsville, headed for Uniontown, in September 1941. The 727 had been built by the West Penn in 1922.

West Penn System

SYSTEM TIME TABLES

West Penn Railways Company
Wheeling Traction Company
Allegheny Valley Street Railway Co.
Ohio Valley Transit Company
Penn Bus Lines

ISSUED JANUARY 1, 1928
Time Tables Subject to Change Without Notice

West Penn Railways

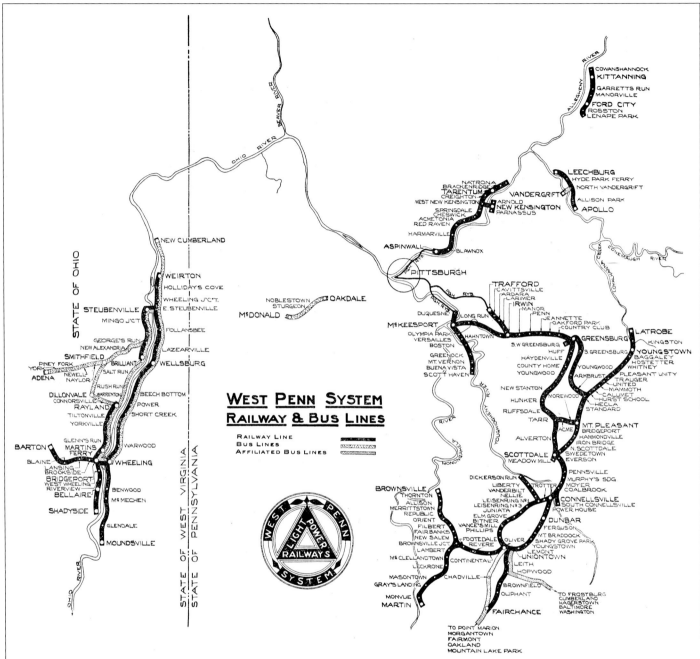

West Penn System Railway & Bus Lines

RAILWAY LINE
BUS LINES
AFFILIATED BUS LINES

Most of West Penn Railways consisted of a network in Allegheny, Westmoreland, and Fayette counties in Pennsylvania. The main line ran from Greensburg, through Hecla (now known as Southwest), Mount Pleasant, Scottdale, Connellsville, and Uniontown, a distance of 31 miles.

There were five non-contiguous lines: 1) Allegheny Valley Street Railway, which paralleled the Allegheny River northeast of Pittsburgh between Aspinwall and Natrona, with a branch crossing the river to serve New Kensington, Parnassus, and Arnold. Service ended in 1937. 2) The Apollo-Leechburg line, operated until 1936 along the north bank of the Kiskiminetas River. 3) The Kittanning line, from Cowanshannock to Kittanning to the Lenape

Park amusement park, which the West Penn built and operated until 1936. This line was standard gauge, the only one not built in Pennsylvania Broad Gauge. 4) Oakdale-McDonald Street Railway, which connected two small communities west of Pittsburgh. It operated until 1927 and was then converted to bus (as is shown on this 1928 map). 5) Wheeling Traction Company (Wheeling, W.Va.). Service operated from Wheeling south to Moundsville, and north to Weirton, on the east bank of the Ohio River. Another line ran on the river's western bank from Shadyside to Rayland, with a branch to Barton, and a connection by bridge to Wheeling. Another branch connected Brilliant and Steubenville to the Wheeling-Weirton line. The West Penn controlled this system from 1906 to 1931.

"Where's the meet?" The motorman of car no. 737 impatiently checks his watch. When the opposing car arrives, he will manually flip the paddles on the box over his head, setting signals to protect his car for a safe run to the next siding. The car is at Lincoln siding, south of Connellsville on the way to Uniontown, on Dec. 8, 1939.

West Penn Railways

Dec. 8, 1939: Trolley car heaven! Two passenger cars and a freight motor meet at Hecla Junction, five miles south of Greensburg, where car no. 737, lightweight no. 840, and a freight motor car meet. The 737 will continue on to Connellsville; the 840 and the freight motor are on the branch to Latrobe.

No. 836, an air brake car that came from West Penn's Allegheny Valley lines, is on the short line to South Connellsville, Aug. 8, 1940.

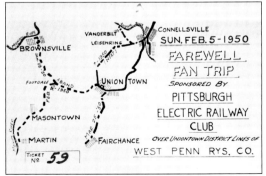

No need for an explanation here!

Wilkes-Barre & Hazleton Railway Company

WB&H Brill-built car no. 228, named "Nuangola," sits idle at the terminal in Wilkes-Barre on July 29, 1933. The railcars got their power from a third rail; the pole was used to enter downtown Hazleton over street trackage of the Lehigh Traction Company. Not long before this photo was taken, no. 228 and her siblings had been replaced by rail buses. Even these would cease service only a few months later as the Great Depression deepened.

T he Wilkes-Barre & Hazleton Railway Company operated a 33-mile third-rail-powered service from Wilkes-Barre to Hazleton, entering Hazleton on two miles of street railway lines of the Lehigh Traction Company. The WB&H ran on its own right-of-way, mostly downgrade from mountain-top Hazleton to Wilkes-Barre on the Lehigh River, remarkably, without a single grade crossing. It made the 31-mile run in 60 minutes.

In the early 1930s, the WB&H replaced its interurban cars with rail buses. These operated until the line was abandoned in September 1933. Freight was also handled. Carloads were interchanged with the "steam railroads" and the electrified Lackawanna & Wyoming Valley (the "Laurel Line," p. 28) at Wilkes-Barre.

Wilkes-Barre & Hazleton Railway Company

THE WILKES BARRE & HAZLETON RAILWAY COMPANY

ADDRESS
ALL COMMUNICATIONS
TO THE COMPANY

HAZLETON, PA. February 7, 1933

Mr. Robert G. Lewis,
359 Gowen Ave., Mt.Airy,
Philadelphia, Penn'a.

Dear Sir:

We have your letter dated February 4, 1933, and
in reply wish to state that we have ceased the operation
of the electric cars between Hazleton and Wilkes-Barre.

These electric cars have been supplanted by a
motor rail-bus which operates on the same rails and under
the same schedule as the former cars. A schedule card is
enclosed for your information.

The only change in this operation is that the
new type rail-buses do not run through the city of Hazleton,
but operate between Hazle Park Jct and Wilkes-Barre. From
Hazleton to Hazle Park Jct we operate a regular highway bus
which meets the rail-buses at Hazle Park Jct in both directions.

We have no special reduced fares for Sundays but
we do have a 50 Trip Commutation Ticket for use between
Hazleton and Wilkes-Barre. This ticket sells at rate of
$37.50 for the 50 trips (25 round trips) and is equivalent
to a 75¢ one-way fare, $1.50 round-trip. ~~Good for~~ Limited to 90 days.

If there is any further information desired, please
let us know.

Yours truly,

WILKES-BARRE AND HAZLETON RAILROAD COMPANY,

E.B.Markle, President & Gen.Mgr.

Sixteen-year-old Bob Lewis, anticipating a visit, wrote to WB&H President & General Manager E. B. Markle in February 1933 asking for information and—always looking to save a buck—inquiring about reduced Sunday fares. Markle tells a lot about the state of his railway in this 1933 letter. Bob, raised as a Quaker, has been described as being "notoriously cheap." He prefers the more-accurate "frugal."

Wilkes-Barre Railway Company

Wilkes-Barre car no. 778 is eastbound on the Dallas line on March 19, 1939, running as a National Railway Historical Society special. The Dallas line had previously extended to Harveys Lake, 25 miles, but had been cut back to Dallas, about 17 miles, at the time this photo was taken. The 778 came to Wilkes-Barre from Pottsville in 1933.

Few Pennsylvania cities the size of Wilkes-Barre—population 86,626 in the 1930 census—had such comprehensive coverage by streetcar lines. With over 100 miles of standard-gauge track and 114 cars on its roster, the Wilkes-Barre Railway Company reached just about all of the communities in the Wyoming Valley. The railway began converting to bus and trolley bus vigorously in 1938. The last streetcar completed its run on Oct. 14, 1950. The final trolley buses ended the era of electric transportation on Oct. 16, 1958.

March 19, 1939: Car no. 772 is southbound at a station on the Nanticoke line; a car for Wilkes-Barre heads north of the opposite track.

York Railways

Y ork Railways served its namesake city well, with local lines in town and suburban lines north to North Haven, northeast to Wrightsville (across the Susquehanna River from Columbia, served by Conestoga Traction Company's line to Lancaster (see p. 12), east to Bittersville, southwest to Hanover (the longest line at 18.5 miles), and northeast to Dover.

The Hanover line was originally constructed with 1,500-volt a.c. trolley wire, but was later converted to 600-volt d.c. to match the voltage on all the other lines.

Streetcar operations ceased on Feb. 4, 1939. All York Railways cars were sold at auction March 14, 1939. York car no. 163, fortunately, is now at the Rockhill Trolley Museum in Rockhill Furnace, Pa., and still operating.

Four Birney cars, one on a National Railway Historical Society charter trip, meet at The Square in downtown York, Dec. 1, 1935.

York Railways

What won't the fans do? On the NRHS charter trip on a cold Dec. 1, 1935, and after much persuasion, York Railways agreed to move open car no. 404 out of the back of the barn for a run to Bittersville. Here, at Lakeview siding, after a brief snow shower, the 404 waits for car no. 326 to clear. Could this be the only photo in existence with an open car operating in the snow?

The crew and a carload of passengers posed for this great photo taken by Conductor Sam Mosmer in 1913. Robert G. Lewis collection.

Closed car no. 327 took over from the 404 to complete the trip on the rest of York Railway's mileage.

York Railways

Car no. 322 is southbound on the Hanover line's long tangent, south of Heidelberg, Feb. 4, 1939, the last day of York Railways service. James P. Shuman photo/William D. Middelton collection.

One week before shutdown, York Railways car no. 325 approaches Spry station on the Windsor line, Jan. 28, 1939. James P. Shuman photo/William D. Middelton collection.

TRUSTEE'S SALE

By order (January 25, 1939) of the District Court of the United States for the Eastern District of Pennsylvania. In the matter of the YORK RAILWAYS COMPANY, in Reorganization, under Section 77-B, Cause No. 20123.

SAMUEL T. FREEMAN & CO., AUCTIONEERS
ESTABLISHED NOVEMBER 12, 1805.

The Entire Equipment
Trolley Cars, Rail, Power Plants, etc.
Relating to the Rail Facilities of the

YORK RAILWAYS CO.
YORK, PA.

TO BE SOLD AT AUCTION

Tuesday, March 14, 1939, at 11 A. M.
ON THE PREMISES

Sale subject to the approval of the Trustee and the Court.

Application for confirmation of the sale will be made before the District Court of the United States for the Eastern District of Pennsylvania, Customs House, Second and Chestnut Streets, Philadelphia, Pa., on Wednesday, March 15, 1939, at 10 A. M.

By order of YORK RAILWAYS COMPANY, Debtor in Possession, Agent of Tradesmens National Bank and Trust Company, Trustee.

SAUL, EWING, REMICK & SAUL, Esqs., Packard Building, Philadelphia, Pa., Counsel for Debtor in Possession.

EVANS, BAYARD & FRICK, Esqs., Land Title Building, Philadelphia, Pa., Counsel for Tradesmens National Bank and Trust Company, Trustee.

SAMUEL T. FREEMAN & CO., Auctioneers
1808-10 CHESTNUT STREET
PHILADELPHIA

27 William Street
New York

80 Federal Street
Boston

95

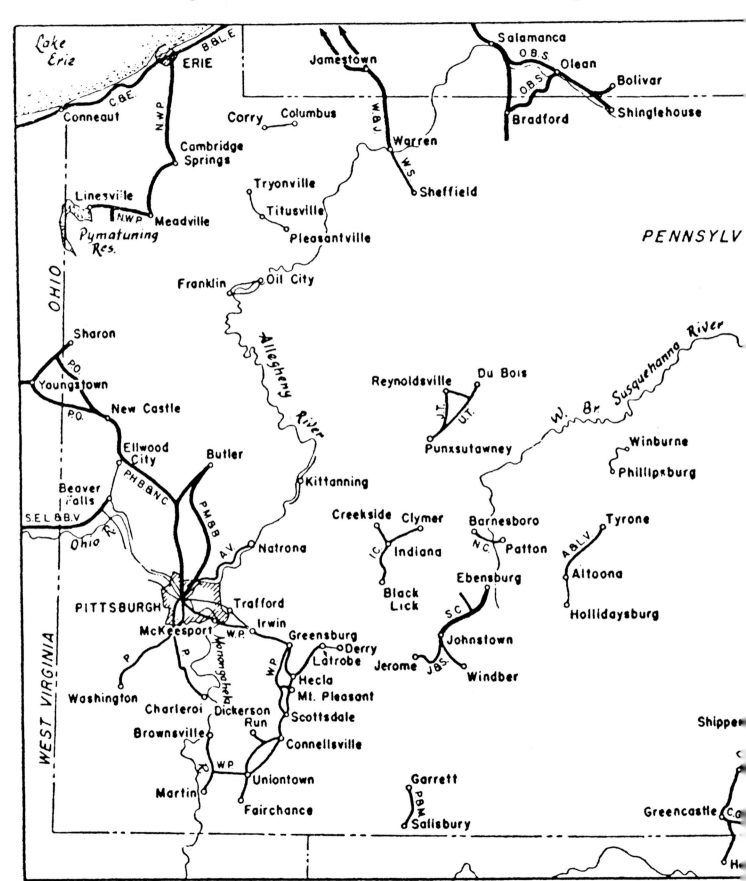

REPRINTED FROM "THE ELECTRIC INTERURBAN RAILWAYS IN AMERICA," GEORGE HILTON AND JOHN DUE, STANFORD UNIVERSITY PRESS, 1964

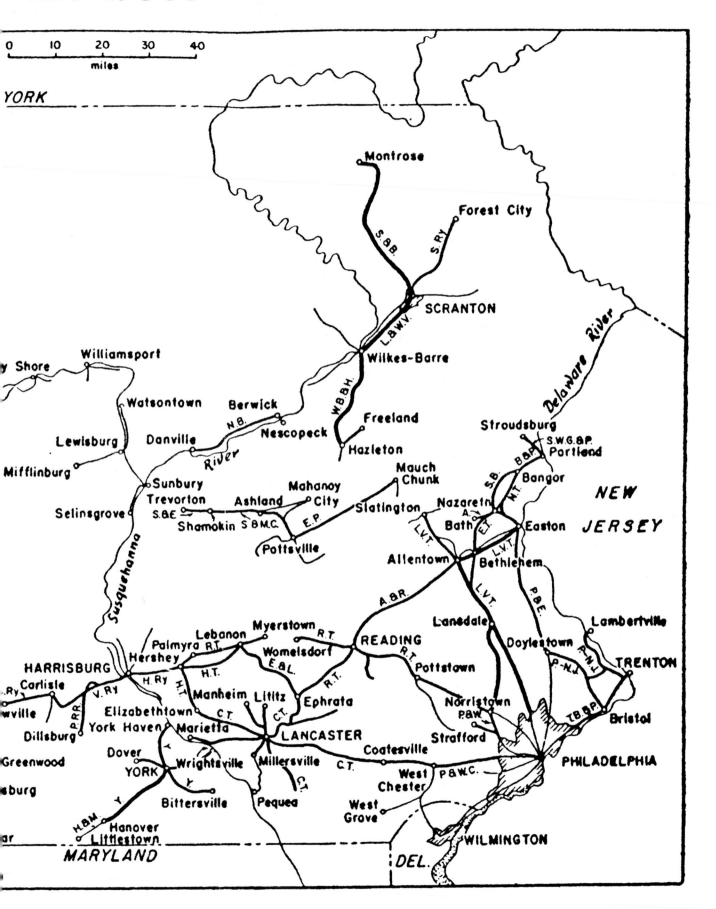

Beyond the Keystone State

Robert G. Lewis's traction photography exploits, as well of those of his many fellow enthusiasts, extended well beyond the borders of his home state of Pennsylvania. The remainder of Keystone State Traction is devoted to a sampling of trolley and interurban systems in 34 U.S. states, Canada and Mexico. Following, in alphabetical order by state, are the best out of an archive of hundreds.

California

October 1945: Sacramento Street Railway car no. 65 awaits a run at the Southern Pacific's Sacramento depot.

Two Pacific Electric PCC-type cars are at Burbank in August 1945. Osgood-Bradley built these cars. D. H. Cope photo/Robert G. Lewis collection.

This Pacific Electric car, seen at Burbank in August 1945, is recruiting women for the U.S. Navy. D. H. Cope photo/Robert G. Lewis collection.

A Market Street Railway 1200 Series car rolls through Burlingame in October 1945.

Pacific Electric club car no. 1209 on the Los Angeles-Newport Beach "Commodore Limited," a 39.7-mile run.

Pacific Electric car no. 1401, at the railway's Los Angeles yard in August 1945, looks like a home-made conversion. Note the hand-painted "U.S. Mail" sign hanging on the nose. D. H. Cope photo/Robert G. Lewis collection.

Sacramento Northern Railway work car no. 403 in an undated photo at the line's shops. D. W. Thickens photo/Robert G. Lewis collection.

San Francisco Market Street Railway Powell Street cable car no. 518 heads uphill in June 1960. The driver of the 1954 Chevy Bel Air seems more than a little impatient!

EFFECTIVE APRIL 3, 1950

PACIFIC ELECTRIC **RAIL SERVICE**

TIME TABLE **2**

LOS ANGELES TERMINAL
Subway Terminal, 423 South Hill Street

LOS ANGELES-GLENDALE-BURBANK LINE

AGENTS
LOS ANGELES—Subway Terminal, 423 So. Hill
St. Phone TU. 7272.
GLENDALE—106 No. Brand Blvd. CItrus 32125
or CItrus 15166.

Sunday Schedule will be operated on New Year's
Day, Memorial Day, Fourth of July, Labor Day,
Thanksgiving Day and Christmas Day.

(Subject to Change Without Notice)

Schedule 2-24

H. O. MARLER
Passenger Traffic Manager
Los Angeles

Oakland: Key System car no. 183 leads a three-car consist out of an F Line tunnel in October 1945.

Pacific Electric car no. 1499, an ex-800-class car, is in work train service in August 1945. It was built by St. Louis Car. D. H. Cope photo/Robert G. Lewis collection.

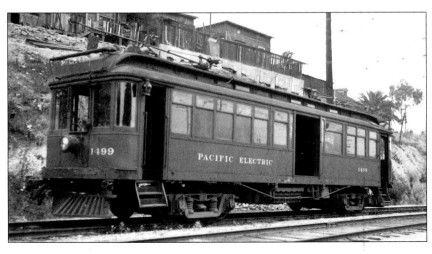

Colorado

September 1937: Southern Colorado Power Company Birney Car no. 132 on the south side of Pueblo.

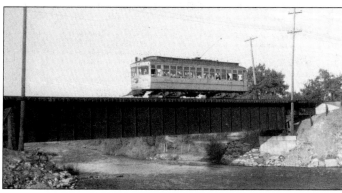

A Denver & Intermountain Railway interurban car crosses Clear Creek on its 15-mile run from Golden.

Denver & Intermountain Railway used a decimal point in numbering its narrow-gauge (3-foot, 6-inch) equipment. Car no. .06 is at Clear Creek Junction on June 12, 1950.

Denver & Intermountain Railway standard-gauge car no. 819 has just come off the loop at Golden in June 1935.

On June 18, 1935, Denver Tramway car no. .05 is sitting just off the loop at Golden.

Connecticut

Bristol Traction Company car no. 4 heads down Bristol's main street in July 1934. The city's total traction mileage was just 11.7 miles.

Delaware

September 1934: Delaware Electric & Power Company was controlled by the Southern Pennsylvania Traction Company. This DE&P car is approaching Penn Station in Wilmington, which today is a primary stop on Amtrak's Northeast Corridor.

A DE&P car, signed "WEST 8TH," heads south in this September 1934 scene.

Idaho

The Utah-Idaho Central Railroad Company operated a 148-mile line that ran north from Ogden, Utah, to Preston, Idaho. U-IC cars nos. 502 and 514 are at Preston on Sept. 9, 1937, ready to depart on a three-hour, 10-minute run to Ogden.

Illinois

The Chicago, North Shore & Milwaukee Railroad's popular Electroliner heads southward through North Chicago Junction in November 1941. These beautiful articulated streamliners were sold to the Philadelphia & Western when the North Shore discontinued service.

This February 1941 timetable introduces the North Shore's "All-Electric Luxury Trains."

Electroliners operated under heavy catenary wiring. This September 1947 scene shows a southbound consist at Lake Bluff, Ill.

Electroliners ARE HERE!

America's First All-Electric Luxury Trains

Five Trips Each Way—Every Day
Between Chicago and Milwaukee

Thrill to an entirely new experience in smooth-flowing travel on swift, silent ELECTROLINERS— the North Shore Line's incomparable new "trains of the future".... in service today!

Here are trains with ultra-modern appointments, luxurious equipment and club-like atmosphere unsurpassed in railroad service. Down to the last minute detail, every facility of the ELECTROLINERS is designed to give you *all-luxury* travel— at regular coach fares—on *all-electric* trains, electrically operated even to temperature control and electro-pneumatic brakes.

RIDE CUSHIONED IN RUBBER!... Nothing has been spared to make the new ELECTROLINERS a triumph in riding comfort. Sweep along easily, silently in spacious *all-electric* trains, completely insulated and sound-proofed to keep out noises.... electrically air-conditioned and heated.... and "cushioned in rubber" at every possible point to give a matchless, quiet, smooth-flowing ride.

NEVER BEFORE TRAINS LIKE THESE! Deep-upholstered seats .... separate smoking lounges .... superbly equipped Tavern-Lounge Cars with softly cushioned settees and unique refreshment appointments .... here indeed is high-speed, all-electric luxury travel .... the first of its kind in America.

Every ELECTROLINER coach is smartly styled by master designers in a different color motif—coral, blue and gold...scarlet and gray...apricot and turquoise. Separate smoking lounges, lens-control illumination, electric air-conditioning and temperature control give you luxury travel at its finest.

Enjoy a perfectly-served "snack" or refreshments in the unique Tavern-Lounge as you glide smoothly over the rails. With its clever murals, its superb appointments, its specially-designed lighting, the distinctive Tavern-Lounge is festive, colorful and inviting! All ELECTROLINER interiors styled and created by James F. Eppenstein and Associates.

EVERY COACH—EVERY DINER-LOUNGE CAR

...beautifully redesigned...on the fast hourly trains between Chicago and Milwaukee

28 trips every day in addition to 5 trips each way by the *Electroliners*

Here is a thrilling fleet of modern, all-electric trains linking Chicago and Milwaukee with fast, frequent all-electric service.

From the fresh, new beauty of car interiors down to their smooth, quiet riding . . . you'll know that here is something decidedly new in fast, clean, comfortable travel!

Electrically controlled heating and ventilation, individual recessed lights over each seat, non-sway safety wheels, rubber flooring laid on felt . . . all assure comfortable, smooth riding. There's always plenty of pure, fresh air . . . heated automatically to just the right temperature regardless of outdoor weather conditions.

Ride these fast, clean, electrified trains. See how beautifully they have been newly designed in every detail for your greater riding comfort!

SMARTLY BEAUTIFUL INTERIORS in the North Shore Line's newly-designed coaches are restful and inviting. Rubber-tiled floor coverings . . . walls, ceilings and equipment done in soft pastel colors . . . luxurious upholstery and soft, perfectly diffused lighting.

FESTIVE DINER-LOUNGE CARS, with colorful cocktail appointments, leave Chicago and Milwaukee morning, noon and evening. Enjoy delicious low-cost meals, prepared by skillful chefs, in colorful, gay surroundings.

The Chicago, Aurora & Elgin Railway's "Wheaton Limited," with car no. 453 trailing, is passed by an inbound train, most likely an equipment extra, at the Marshfield Station on the Garfield Park elevated line in Chicago, circa 1947.

March 13, 1954: Chicago Transit Authority car no. 336 is at the intersection of Clark Street and Archer Avenue.

Chicago Transit Authority PCC-type car no. 4020 is seen in April 1948 at 64th St and Stony Island.

Illinois Terminal car no. 1203 southbound on Center Street at the intersection of Jefferson Street in Bloomington, September 1952. Service through Bloomington ended less than a year later.

March 1954: Chicago Transit Authority car no. 296 is southbound on Kedzie Avenue, having just passed beneath the Garfield Park "L" (elevated railway) in the background. The elevated structure was torn down in 1958 and the tracks were relocated into the median of the Congress (now Eisenhower) Expressway. By that time, streetcar operation on Kedzie Avenue (and throughout Chicago) had been discontinued.

A Chicago North Shore & Milwaukee three-car train, led by no. 161, is southbound on a gauntlet track in Glencoe, Ill. The sign on no. 161's nose reads "CHICAGO EXPRESS, SHORE LINE ROUTE."

Indiana

Until 1970, the eastern end of the Chicago South Shore & South Bend's trackage was this modest-sized yard just east of the St. Joseph River on the fringe of downtown South Bend. Now operated by the Northern Indiana Commuter Transportation District, trains terminate at South Bend Airport, located on the city's west side. This view is from October 1943.

Bob Lewis (right), with Indiana Service Corporation General Manager Bill Powelson and a special car, touring the Fort Wayne system in October 1943.

May 1948: CSS&SB car no. 28 leads a two-car consist southbound through East Chicago, headed for South Bend.

The CSS&SB also hauled freight. An eastbound doubleheader holds the siding between Michigan City and Gary in 1949, waiting for a Chicago-bound passenger train. CSS&SB freight thrives today, still under its own name, as a division of Anacostia & Pacific Company.

Indiana

Hartford City, Sept. 18, 1939: The Indiana Railroad (not to be confused with today's short line Indiana Rail Road) was the state's largest interurban, with Indianapolis its main hub. The city's huge "Traction Terminal," opened in 1904, grew to become the largest interurban railway terminal in the world. At its peak, this terminal hosted seven million passengers a year, and 500 interurban trains a day, from all over Indiana. The Indiana Railroad ceased operations in 1941.

August 1943: "Traction Light" Indiana Service Corporation car no. 817 is in work train service southbound, just north of its Fort Wayne home turf. No. 817 is the former Toledo & Chicago no. 8.

Iowa

Fort Dodge, Des Moines & Southern car no. 82, built by the Niles Car Company in 1907, is at Boone in September 1953.

Des Moines Railway car no. 726 at Urbandale on the Fair Ground Line, Jan. 31, 1948. W. H. Schmidt, II photo/Robert G. Lewis collection.

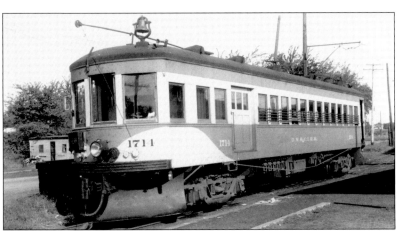

Des Moines & Central Iowa's huge combine car no. 1714, with snow plow ready, poses at Perry in 1947.

Fort Dodge, Des Moines & Southern car no. 66, like no. 82 built by the Niles Car Company in 1907, is at Fort Dodge in September 1953. No. 66 was scrapped in 1956.

Waterloo, Cedar Falls & Northern Railway car no. 100 at the Cedar Falls station in May 1948. W. H. Schmidt, II photo/Robert G. Lewis collection.

Waterloo, Cedar Falls & Northern Railway car no. 373, an ex-Knoxville, Tenn., car, loads passengers at Waterloo depot on Mulberry Street in May 1948. Car no. 141 (right) is most likely holding down Waterloo-Waverly service, its usual assignment. W. H. Schmidt, II photo/Robert G. Lewis collection.

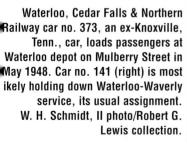

Waterloo, Cedar Falls & Northern Railway car no. 100 at Denver, Iowa, in May 1950.

WCF&N rolling stock at the Waterloo Shops, May 1948. The railway operated a small fleet of electric transfer locomotives. The turntable in the foreground is unusual for an electrified railway. W. H. Schmidt, II photo/Robert G. Lewis collection.

Kentucky

Cincinnati, Newport & Covington Railway car no. 513, running on Route no. 1 (note the pilot placard), at South Fort Mitchell, March 30, 1941.

A CN&C Railway car heads for Newport, across the Ohio River from Cincinnati, in October 1948.

A Louisville Railways car heads for downtown Louisville along South Park Street, Sept. 17, 1936.

Louisiana

New Orleans Public Service car no. 932 is on Canal Street, just south of Union Station, in June 1952.

New Orleans Public Service car no. 956 on the Claiborne line in June 1952.

Maryland

Baltimore Transit monitor roof car no. 5593 is westbound at Dickeyville, crossing Route 35, February 1952.

Baltimore Transit car no. 5745 is running eastbound on Route 9 out of Ellicott City, May 1954.

Washington, Baltimore & Annapolis car no. 50 is at Naval Academy Junction on its run from Annapolis, July 1935.

Massachusetts

Eastern Massachusetts Street Railway car no. 4251 at Quincy, May 20, 1935.

Union Street Railway car no. 610 at Lund's Corner, New Bedford, October 13, 1943. Osgood-Bradley built the 610 in 1929; it was sold to New York City's Queensboro Bridge Line in 1949. William H. Watts, II, photo/Robert G. Lewis collection.

Eastern Massachusetts Street Railway cars nos. 6064 (left) and 6058 meet at Holbrook, May 26, 1935

Worcester Street Railway car no. 956 on Providence Street, Providence, Rhode Island, June 6, 1933. William H. Watts, II, photo/Robert G. Lewis collection.

"Ride all day for $1—20 cities and 51 towns": Eastern Massachusetts Street Railway car no. 6025 at North Andover, May 26, 1935.

Holyoke Street Railway steam coach roof car no 124, at Holyoke, July 20, 1934.

Minnesota

Twin Cities Rapid Transit cars had a large open, but gated, rear platform to expedite discharge of passengers, as well as a monitor roof. This scene is from May 21, 1950. The sign stenciled on the rear says "STOP 10 FEET BACK REQUIRED BY LAW."

Twin Cities Rapid Transit Car no. 1301 is on the wye at Hopkins, ready for its return to downtown Minneapolis. Note the large, net-like fender protruding from the nose.

Missouri

A Kansas City Public Service PCC car heads eastward across the city's short elevated line in April 1948.

KCPS PCC car no. 521 has just dropped a passenger off at a station on Route 53 on the 56 "Country Club" line in April 1948.

A little further down Kansas City's elevated track, a KCPS car is about to enter an enclosed station in April 1948.

Montana

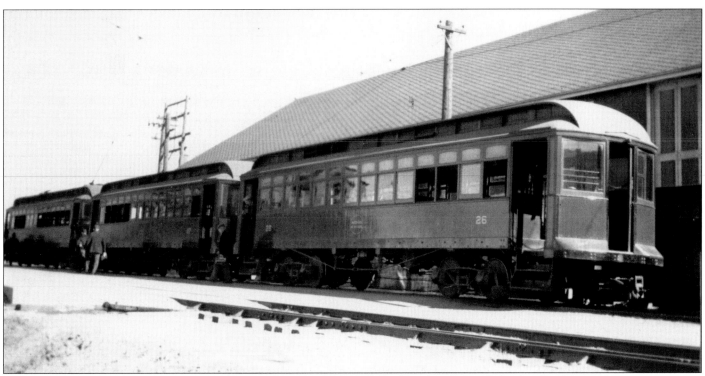

Anaconda Street Railway car no. 16 on its smelter line, Sept. 17, 1938. F. W. Moulder photo/Robert G. Lewis collection.

Nebraska

Omaha & Council Bluffs Street Railway car no. 1008 slows for passengers near Omaha's Union Station, November 1951.

New Jersey

Public Service of New Jersey car no. 2255 at Bound Brook, the south end of its long run from Newark, January 1933. William H. Watts, II, photo/Robert G. Lewis collection.

It's *not* a PCC: Atlantic City & Shore Railroad Company car no. 6891 may look like a PCC, but actually was built to the railway's specifications by Brill. "Brilliner" 6891 is at the north end of the line at "Inlet," Atlantic City, in summer 1939.

⟫"SHORE FAST LINE"⟫

RAIL AND BUS AUTUMN TIME TABLE
Subject to Change Without Notice
In Effect November 10, 1935

HIGH SPEED ELECTRIC TRAINS
Between

ATLANTIC CITY
TERMINAL AT BOARDWALK & VIRGINIA AVE., and

Pleasantville - Northfield - Linwood - Somers Point

OCEAN CITY
TERMINAL AT BOARDWALK AND EIGHTH ST.

In Atlantic City cars can be boarded at Virginia Ave. and
the Boardwalk and at all street stops on Atlantic Ave.
between Virginia Ave. and Mississippi Ave.

75c – Daily Excursion – 75c
ATLANTIC CITY — OCEAN CITY
Good on All Trains
Either Direction—ONE DAY ROUND TRIP—Rail Only
Sold at Ticket Offices and by Conductors on Ocean City Div. Cars

Atlantic Avenue and Longport Trolleys to
INLET, VENTNOR, MARGATE AND LONGPORT

Public Service of New Jersey car no. 2121, "Union City," on the elevated line out of Hoboken, Feb. 12, 1935.

Public Service of New Jersey "City Subway" (today's NJ Transit Newark Light Rail) car no. 3213 leaves the Heller Parkway stop, bound for downtown Newark, on Nov. 3, 1936. Thirty years later, co-author William C. Vantuono would be riding PCC cars on this line as a boy, with his father and sister, on Saturday outings to Branch Brook Park.

Feb. 2, 1936: Atlantic City & Shore car no. 103 is halfway across the long wooden trestle connecting Somers Point with Ocean City.

Sept. 7, 1936: Atlantic City & Shore cars 117 and 114, running in multiple-unit, arrive at Pleasantville, headed for Ocean City.

New York

May 17, 1936: Fonda, Johnstown & Gloversville car no. 45 has just started the return trip from the end of its run at Lyons, and is headed south for Amsterdam.

International Railways car no. 4004 parallels the New York Central on a run to Lockport, May 31, 1937.

May 17, 1936: FJ&G car no. 60 has just passed lightweight "Bullet" car no. 125 on a passing track at Fort Johnson.

The Jamestown, Westfield & Northwestern Railroad Company operated a single-track line 32.5 miles south from Westfield, on Lake Erie, to Jamestown. Big interurban car no. 301 is midway between the two terminals on July 21, 1936.

May 30, 1937: International Railways car no. 3018 is at Riverview, the terminus of one of its local lines serving the city of Niagara Falls.

Schenectady Railway car no. 693 at Crescent Park, Schenectady, Aug. 31, 1931. William H. Watts, II photo/Robert G. Lewis collection.

CORRECTED TO APRIL 27, 1930

CHAUTAUQUA
JAMESTOWN WESTFIELD AND NORTH WESTERN R.R.
LAKE ROUTE

TIME TABLES

LOCAL AND CONDENSED

Showing Through Train Connections With

Buffalo	Pittsburgh
Rochester	Cleveland
Syracuse	Detroit
Albany	Chicago
New York	Cincinnati
Boston	St. Louis

NEW YORK CENTRAL LINES

Via Westfield, N. Y.

AND

PRR

Via Mayville, N. Y.

RAILROAD AND PULLMAN TICKETS
TO ALL POINTS

ALL UNION STATIONS   NO TRANSFER

MODERN ALL STEEL EQUIPMENT

EASTERN STANDARD TIME

Jamestown, Westfield & Northwestern car no. 302 is at Jamestown on July 21, 1946.

A New York Railways monitor-roof car, running on third rail, is westbound on the 86th Street crosstown line through Central Park—abandoned less than one month after this photo was taken on May 5, 1936. Note the sidewalk cleaner at left. Each was issued a cart, and assigned a city block to keep clean. They were dubbed "Whitewings" for the jackets they wore.

International Railways car no. 3018, equipped with Brill Maximum Traction trucks, is at the Niagara Falls station, May 1937. The Maximum Traction truck's unique design placed the majority of the car's weight on larger, motor-driven inner wheelsets, while the smaller outer wheelset turned the truck as it negotiated curves. This arrangement allowed for a longer car with only two driven axles and increased rail adhesion.

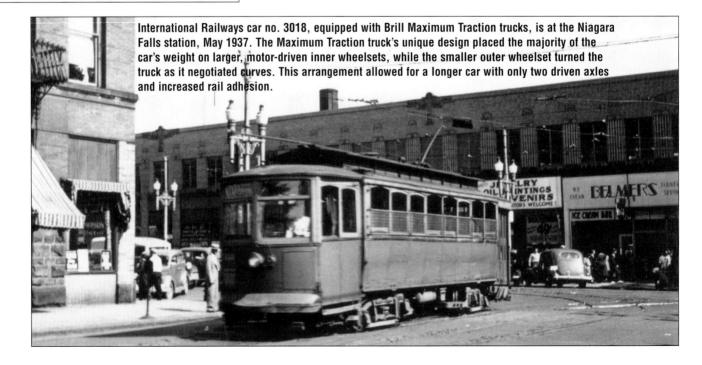

North Carolina

Duke Power Company car no. 55 stops to discharge a passenger in Charlotte in September 1937. J. H. Lewis photo/Robert G. Lewis collection.

Left: Piedmont & Northern two-car train, with car no. 2103 leading, is westbound out of Charlotte in September 1937. J. H. Lewis photo/Robert G. Lewis collection. Below: P&N electric motor no. 351 heads two former Pennsylvania Railroad coaches at the line's Greenwood, S.C., station in August 1951.

Tidewater Power & Light (Wilmington) car no. 63 at Wrightsville Beach, November 1938.

Not many cities had inclined planes for their streetcars. Cincinnati Street Railway car no. 2470 on Route 49 (200 to Eden Park) gets a lift up Mt. Adams on March 30, 1941. Bob Lewis shot this photo from a car on its way down.

One of Cleveland Railways Company's big center-door cars, signed "CLIFTON-PUBLIC SQUARE," is eastbound along Clifton Blvd., Oct. 19, 1941.

Cincinnati & Lake Erie wasn't just streamliners. Two freight motors, with no. 622 leading, are at their loading dock in Columbus, Sept. 19, 1936.

Cincinnati Steet Railway PCC car no. 1154 at the Warsaw-Price Hill loop, October 1948.

Shaker Heights Rapid Transit maintenance-of-way car OX is working on the right-of-way just east of Cleveland Union Terminal, October 1953.

Above: Cincinnati, Newport & Covington Railway Company single-truck car no. 326 at the end of its run in Covington, Ky. This car was not equipped with air brakes; the motorman wound the brakes to a stop by hand—a rare thing when this photo was taken in March 1941. Note the Ex-Lax and Coca-Cola signs in the drugstore window. Below: Akron Transport center-door car no. 2018 on East Market Street, Akron, Sept. 19, 1936.

Cincinnati Street Railway monitor-roof car no. 951 on Route 34 in downtown Cincinnati, March 30, 1941.

Oklahoma

Above: Sand Springs Railway car no. 76 begins its run outside Tulsa Union Station, Oct. 4, 1950. The Sand Springs ran from its namesake town to Tulsa, a distance of 10 miles. It was owned and operated by a local orphanage. Left: Boxcar no. 123, one of eight, waits for a load at a siding in Sand Springs. Not many electric railways owned freight cars for interchange with Class I railroads. The Sand Springs owned 18.

Oregon

OK, it's a modern street car, but we figured we'd give you at least one example of the growing number of American cities that have rediscovered the electric street railway. This articulated three-unit car was built by Skoda in the Czech Republic for Portland Streetcar, which is operated by the Tri-County Metropolitan Transportation District of Oregon. No. 001 pictured here was photographed by Bob Lewis's brother Hans in March 2004, soon after it was placed into service. Tri-Met also operates an extensive light rail system.

Rhode Island

What's playing at The Strand on East Avenue (near Main Street) in Pawtucket, as United Electric Railway car no. 1049 glides by on March 3, 1932? Why, it's none other than Marion Davies and Robert Montgomery in "Blondie of the Follies." William H. Watts, II photo/Robert G. Lewis collection.

United Electric Railway work car no. 1529 at the power house at Riverview Station, Aug. 18, 1935. Roger Borrup photo/Robert G. Lewis collection.

United Electric Railway car no. 1324 southbound at Horsie, April 21, 1934. William H. Watts, II photo/Robert G. Lewis collection.

Tennessee

Tennessee Electric Power Company car no. 233 climbs uphill on Missionary, Chattanooga, Sept. 27, 1939.

A Tennessee Electric Power
Company car descends on
Chattanooga's Mount
Lookout Incline Railway,
Sept. 27, 1939.

Texas

Dallas Railway & Terminal Company double-end car no. 755 is just east of Dallas Union Station, May 1948.

Houston North Shore car no. 522 at the McCarty Avenue terminal, Houston, May 1948. Note the "Missouri Pacific Lines" lettering. When Bob Lewis took this photo, he took a MoPac bus from Houston Union Station to McCarty Avenue, then the railway to Baytown and Goose Creek. The 26.2-mile line was abandoned later in 1948.

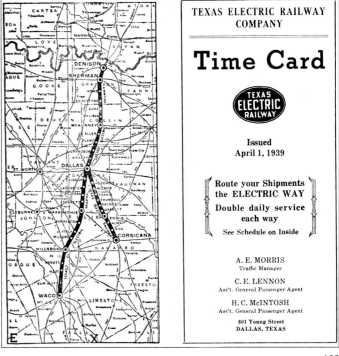

Utah

Wide-open spaces: Bamberger Electric Railway car no. 125 is midway on its 36-mile run from Ogden to Salt Lake City. The Brill-built car came from the Fonda, Johnstown & Gloversville (p. 124). Photographer unknown/Robert G. Lewis collection.

Utah-Idaho Central Railway's mixed train leaves Fairview, Idaho, on its 88.7-mile run to Ogden, in September 1937.

Vermont

July 21, 1934: Springfield Terminal Railway combine car no. 16 heads for Charleston, where it will connect with the Central Vermont Railway.

Springfield Terminal Railway line car no. 8 just east of Springfield, July 20, 1934.

Virginia

Richmond-Ashland Railway Company car no. 319 is arriving at its Richmond terminal on a short stretch of elevated track in November 1935. The line had been planned to continue north to Washington D.C., but never got further than Ashland, a distance of 18 miles.

Virginia Electric & Power nos. 417 and 419 meet at Centralia siding on the Petersburg line, Nov. 11, 1935. William H. Watts, II photo/Robert G. Lewis collection.

Arlington & Fairfax car no. 314 is at the end of its route at Fairfax, Oct. 27, 1935.

Virginia

Arlington & Fairfax car no. 307 and motor car no. 105 at Rosslyn, 1936.

A Virginia Electric & Power car, signed "NAVAL BASE," rolls down a Norfolk street, July 18, 1934. William H. Watts, II photo/Robert G. Lewis collection.

Virginia Electric & Power double truck Birney car no. 419, in the foreground, meets a southbound car at Hull Street and the Petersburg Turnpike in Richmond, Nov. 24, 1935. No. 419 was unusual, as nearly all Birney cars were single truck.

Capital Transit car no. 723 is approaching Washington, D.C. Union Station at 13th and D Streets, May 30, 1936.

Transit NEWS

Washington, D. C.　　　February, 1937

CAPITAL TRANSIT
FARES AND TRANSFERS
DISTRICT OF COLUMBIA

Fares in General:

On all street car lines and on bus and "owl" bus lines first listed below the fare is:

Cash, 10 cents.
Tokens, 7½ cents; sold 4 for 30 cents.
School tickets 3 cents, sold in books of 10 tickets for 30 cents or 40 tickets for $1.20. School tickets are of two kinds: day tickets good for transportation only to and from school between the hours of 7 A. M. and 7 P. M.; night tickets good between the hours of 4 P. M. and 11 P. M. Neither are good on Saturdays, Sundays or holidays. All are sold on identification attested by teacher, to pupils under 18 years of age, of public, parochial, high schools and private schools approved by the Public Utilities Commission.

D. C. Weekly Pass, $1.25, good for unlimited riding by bearer from 5 A. M. one Sunday to 5 A. M. the following Sunday on all street car lines and on all Company bus lines where the unit fare is 10 cents or less. With the pass 2 children under 12 may be taken along free by pass bearer on Sundays and holidays.

Capital Traction Company car no. 182 at Union Station, Nov. 6, 1934. Capital Traction and Capital Transit (above) were the two major street railway companies in Washington, D.C. at the time. Capital Traction was the smaller of the two.

Washington Railway & Electric car no. 762 on the Cabin John Line in Potomac Heights, Sept. 3, 1931. William H. Watts, II photo/Robert G. Lewis collection.

Washington State

On a typically overcast day in July 1937, North Coast Transportation Company interurban car no. 55 is holding the main at a passing siding midway between Seattle and Everett.

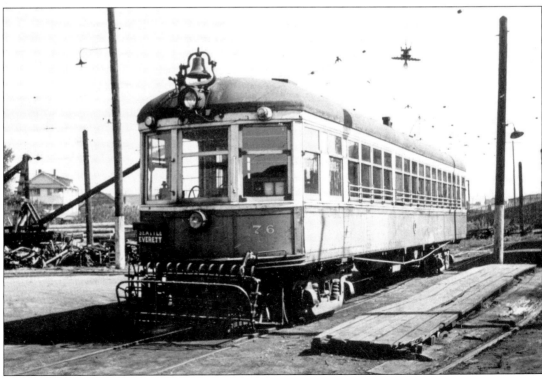

September 1937: North Coast car no. 76 is at Everett, the railway's northern terminus, 29 miles up the coast from Seattle.

West Virginia

Cooperative Transit of Wheeling car no. 48 (ex-Wheeling Traction 648, built by Cincinnati Car Company in 1924), rolls through downtown Wheeling, Feb. 22, 1936.

Charleston Interurban Railroad car no. 32 is at a substation turnout, St. Albans, July 25, 1936.

Panhandle Traction Company car no. 751 is southbound at Warwood on a 90-minute interstate run from Weirton, Ohio to Wheeling, Feb. 22, 1936.

Cooperative Transit car no. 67 on interstate run from Barton, Ohio to Wheeling, Oct. 12, 1941.

Wisconsin

Now operating for Kenosha Motor Coach Lines, former Milwaukee Electric Railway & Transport Company car no. 1144 is near the Public Service Building in downtown Milwaukee, July 1949. Note the abundance of new postwar automobiles jamming the street. The taxicab trundling in the opposite direction is a 1949 Ford. To the right can be seen the double trolley wire used by the city's fleet of "trackless trolleys," otherwise known as electric trolley buses.

Transit Guide

MILWAUKEE
Metropolitan Area

..WHERE TO GO AND
HOW TO GET THERE
By

STREET RAILWAY
TRACKLESS TROLLEY
MOTOR BUS *and*
Local **RAPID TRANSIT**

KEEP THIS GUIDE FOR READY REFERENCE

It contains a map of Milwaukee and suburbs with (1) Street
names, (2) House numbering and (3) Transportation lines
(street car, trackless trolley, motorbus and Local Rapid
Transit) clearly indicated; also, information on Rates of Fare,
Places of interest and a map of the Rapid Transit interurban railway and bus system serving south-eastern Wisconsin.

THE TRANSPORT CO.
THE MILWAUKEE ELECTRIC RAILWAY & TRANSPORT CO.

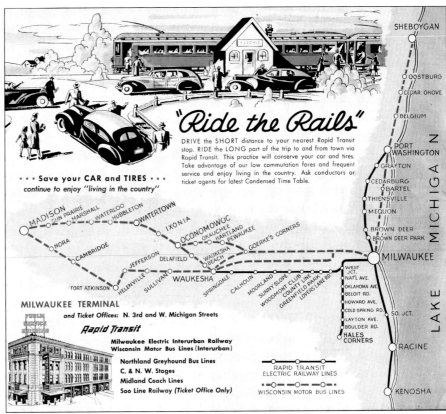

"Ride the Rails"

DRIVE the SHORT distance to your nearest Rapid Transit
stop. RIDE the LONG part of the trip to and from town via
Rapid Transit. This practice will conserve your car and tires.
Take advantage of our low commutation fares and frequent
service and enjoy living in the country. Ask conductors or
ticket agents for latest Condensed Time Table.

• • • Save your CAR and TIRES • • •
continue to enjoy "living in the country"

MILWAUKEE TERMINAL

and Ticket Offices: N. 3rd and W. Michigan Streets

Rapid Transit

Milwaukee Electric Interurban Railway
Wisconsin Motor Bus Lines (Interurban)

Northland Greyhound Bus Lines
C. & N. W. Stages
Midland Coach Lines
Soo Line Railway (Ticket Office Only)

RAPID TRANSIT
ELECTRIC RAILWAY LINES

WISCONSIN MOTOR BUS LINES

A Kenosha Motor Coach
Lines interurban car nears
the end of its run at Racine,
Wisc., in July 1947. William
H. Schmidt, II photo/Robert
G. Lewis collection.

Milwaukee Electric Railway
& Transport Company at
West Limits, Waukesha,
Sept. 9, 1939.

Canada

Montreal & Southern Counties car no. 610 leads a two-car train south through St. Lambert, Quebec, in June 1927. Photographer unknown/Robert G. Lewis collection.

Winnipeg Electric Company car no. 354 is southbound on its double-track right-of-way paralleling Broadway, October 1950.

No. 69

In effect April 26th, 1931
En vigueur le 26 Avril, 1931

TRAVEL THE ELECTRIC WAY

SAFETY FIRST

MONTREAL & SOUTHERN COUNTIES RAILWAY

EASTERN STANDARD TIME
HEURE SOLAIRE

Complete Time Card
OF
Suburban and Interurban Service

Horaire complet des trains Suburbains et Interurbains

Train times are not guaranteed.
Les heures des trains ne sont pas garanties.

MONTREAL & SOUTHERN COUNTIES RAILWAY COMPANY

Terminal Station, Corner McGill & Youville Streets
Terminus, coins McGill et Youville

Montreal Tramways cars pass our Terminal Station at Montreal.
Les tramways passent près de notre Terminus à Montréal.

Bell Tel.
PLateau 1144
MArquette 6650

W. B. POWELL
General Manager
Gérant Général

Bob Lewis' Railway Age colleague William H. Schmidt, II photographed this Ottawa Electric Railway Company car on a wintry day in January 1948. Robert G. Lewis collection.

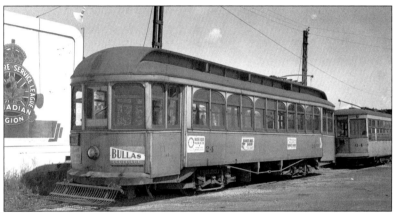

Kitchner & Waterloo Street Railway wooden interurban car no. 24, with a Birney car behind it, is at the railway's Kitchner, Ontario, car shop in September 1946.

Toronto Transit Commission car no. 112 rolls through Richmond Hill, Ontario, Dec. 4, 1938.

A Montreal & Southern Counties car, signed "LACHINE," heads south from Montreal, Sept. 5, 1951.

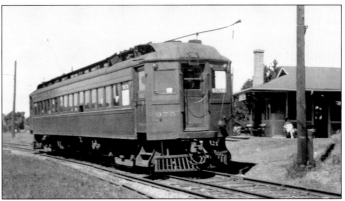

Grand River Railway car no. 975 is at Kitchner Junction, Ontario, September 1946.

Sandwich, Windsor & Amherstberg Railway car no. 452 at Sandwich, Ontario, Sept. 15, 1936.

Lake Erie & Northern Railway interurban car no. 844 is enroute between Brantford and Paris, Ontario, July 1954.

Hamilton Street Railway car no. 417 is operating a National Railway Historical Society special in September 1947.

Mexico

Mexico City's Servicio de Transportes Eléctricos (STE) car no. 221, a 1908 Mexico Tramways Company (MTC) product, in June 1952. Much of Mexico City's streetcar system was built and operated by MTC. In 1945, the Mexican government accused MTC of poor service and broken contracts, confiscated its property and formed a new agency, Servicio de Transportes Urbanos y Suburbanos, to operate the service. The latter was reorganized as STE in 1947, but MTC did not give up control completely until January 1952. STE still operates the city's remaining streetcars, as well as electric trolley buses.

Above: STE steam-coach-roofed car no. 818, signed "OBREGON," is on Route 91 in June 1952. The 800-series cars operated on Mexico City's suburban lines for many years, beginning with an MTC order for 25 cars from St. Louis Car in 1907. Other orders followed; MTC built and rebuilt duplicates at its Indianilla shops.

Left: In 1952, Vera Cruz Traction Company was still operating single truck open cars. Bob Lewis took this photo on a rainy day in June of that year.

Johnstown Traction Company car no. 249, one of five cars built by Brill in 1901 and numbered 247-251, at Dale in 1939. That's a Galliker's Ice Cream truck in the background. Galliker's is still in business. The streetcars are long gone.